SECRETS OF THE
ZEN BUSINESS WARRIOR

Advance Praise

"*Secrets of the Zen Business Warrior* is a great read for those who want to learn more about a unique perspective on how to grow a business while living the day-to-day with fun, joy and equilibrium."

— **Tony Hsieh,** CEO of Zappos.com & *New York Times* Best Selling Author of *Delivering Happiness*

"Lina's book, *Secrets of the Zen Business Warrior*, will provide you the clarity, passion, and principles you need to take your life to the next level, to the level you heart desires."

— **Janet Bray Attwood**, New York Times Bestselling Author, *The Passion Test* and *Your Hidden Riches*

"*If only this book landed in my hands thirty years ago!*

In her book, Lina was able to organize a life's wisdom in an entertaining, crystal clear and heartfelt way that makes it hard to stop reading. Throughout the book, there is wonderful mix of her life´s story, deep and insightful principles, real life anecdotes, easy to follow ideas, and steps that will inspire you to eagerly move toward a passionate life with purpose and boldness.

Actually, this book can help any person, whatever his role or profession. It can be life-changing for entrepreneurs and employees as well as housewives, students, or retired individuals.

The wisdom throughout *Secrets of the Zen Business Warrior* can help anyone live a life in such a way that when the time comes and the "whistle is blown at the end of the game" one can look back and say "mission accomplished" and feel peace, fulfillment, and joy."

— **Dana Benarroch**, Founder ConTacto Humano Organizacional, Enterprise Transformational Coach and Speaker Top 50 Leading Enterprises Transformational Coach—Colombia

"Lina is an inspirational woman leader generous to share all her wisdom. In a very simple, down to earth, and easy to read approach, this book takes you on a seven-step journey that will dramatically transform your personal and professional life.

Success: all starts from within!"

— **David Legher**, Senior Vice President/President
AVON South Latin America

"As founders and eager determined entrepreneurs, we strongly believe in the need for maintaining healthy balance and preserving our company's founding purpose, perspective, and energy, while the inner you acts and maintains agility to sustain success.

Lina's book is an instrumental book for business owners and leaders, written from experience and the daily learning process.

You need the *Secrets of the Zen Business Warrior*!"

— **Lionel Carrasco** and **Marcela Henao**,
Founders, CEO & CMO, Leap Factor,
Awarded 2014 Endeavor Most Innovative Company,
Awarded 2017 Fastest Growing Technology Company Florida

"*Secrets of the Zen Business Warrior.* Seven steps to become a successful entrepreneur. Each step with its own metric and a proposal on how to guarantee success before taking the next step.

Lina Betancur shows us throughout the book the importance of the *self*, where emotional skills top cognitive skills in the race for success. She digs into her own positive and challenging life experiences, as a source to inspire the reader and as proof of her teachings' proven path."

— **Alejandro Ceballos Zuluaga,**
Former CEO, Orbitel S.A, Leonisa International S.A.

"It is difficult to find a book for entrepreneurs that will not solely be centered around theories, strategies, or processes that inevitably make us—business owners—think that we need to have a lot of certifications and studies to make our business succeed in the long run…when in fact, success is really about balance of what is most important in our lives: health, love, abundance, fun! I truly loved reading and learning from Lina Betancur new ways to grow and enjoy my business and personal life to the fullest."

— **Claudia Valencia Cordoba,**
Business Owner/CEO, SUMEL S.A.S

"I read this book in one day. I felt inspired by her courage, admired of her frankness and identified with her because I have faced and continue to face some of the challenges she has referred to us on this engaging report of her journey so far."

— **Andres Restrepo Isaza**, CEO, Mineros S.A.

"Wow! I just read a book so entertaining I almost forgot that I was also learning lessons about business. *Secrets of the Zen Business Warrior* by Lina Betancur is like talking to a dear friend who just happens to have the experience and knowledge of a seasoned CEO and the humility and insight of what else—a Zen warrior! Using anecdotes from her life, Lina guides us through the very attainable process of regaining passion in our work lives. It's concise and practical yet inspires a deeper soul searching than the typical business achievement how-to book. I'm looking forward to more books by this author!"

— **Lea Esquenazi**, Co-Founder, Advanced Female Care

"Even though this book is geared toward entrepreneurs bootstrapping a business, it will still resonate with anyone who is trying to clear-cut a path in their life to a more successful and happy self. Lina Betancur's story of having to start and restart both her business and her life during her 30's, a time which you think everything should already be laid out and on cruise control is inspiring. It's not the time period you expect upheaval and extreme life changes. The author leads us through this period in her life, and shares with us the knowledge she gained that led to her current success with dynamic language bristling with energy that makes you want to burst into action yourself. She encourages you to write your own story, a key method for self-assessment, and also a valuable tool that will show you if you are being honest, especially with yourself. If you're having trouble seeing the forest for the trees, this book is like a big machete."

— **David Osorio,** Writer

SECRETS OF THE

ZEN

BUSINESS
WARRIOR

7 Steps to Grow Your Business,
Feel Excited, and Stay Motivated, *AGAIN*

LINA BETANCUR

NEW YORK

LONDON • NASHVILLE • MELBOURNE • VANCOUVER

SECRETS OF THE ZEN BUSINESS WARRIOR

7 Steps to Grow Your Business, Feel Excited, and Stay Motivated, *AGAIN*

© 2020 **LINA BETANCUR**

Published in New York, New York, by Morgan James Publishing in partnership with Difference Press. Morgan James is a trademark of Morgan James, LLC. www.MorganJamesPublishing.com

ISBN 978-1-64279-456-4 paperback
ISBN 978-1-64279-457-1 eBook
Library of Congress Control Number: 2019931648

In an effort to support local communities, raise awareness and funds, Morgan James Publishing donates a percentage of all book sales for the life of each book to Habitat for Humanity Peninsula and Greater Williamsburg.

Get involved today! Visit
www.MorganJamesBuilds.com

DEDICATION

To David.
What a magnificent journey it has been with you in my life.

TABLE OF CONTENTS

Zen: [zen] noun

    It is a state of calm attentiveness in which one's actions are guided by intuition (a.k.a. your heart) rather than by conscious effort.

    Zen involves dropping illusion and seeing things without distortion created by your own thoughts.

The Zen Business Warrior: noun

    The path to conquer one's self.

FOREWORD

Attention entrepreneurs who want the real inside track to total success.

Lina's *Secrets of the Zen Business Warrior* is a stand out pragmatic gem for new and seasoned business leaders.

What's exceptionally powerful are the life and business lessons Lina candidly shares from her vast experience that will shed deep light on the inner psychology of what works and doesn't as you climb your success ladder.

She goes deep into the inner workings of intention and mindset with new clarity and touching wisdom.

Don't just read this, devour it with care and presence and watch how you'll skip years of turmoil and attain greater success all with inner fulfillment and the sharpness of a Zen Warrior.

— Satyen Raja, Founder WarriorSage Trainings,
www.WarriorSage.com

INTRODUCTION

WHO IS THIS BOOK FOR?

This book is for the brave entrepreneur who did not settle for less in his/her life than the freedom, growth, and fulfillment that a successful business has the potential to provide.

Some individuals have a clear idea or vision about the type of business they want and the future it holds for them from the very beginning; for some people, circumstances just sort of push them into it. It does not matter how it started, what is most important is that you are there: you have a business running.

You have worked hard, very hard, to make it succeed. You might have reached that always expanding goal—or maybe you haven't yet. You have a commitment, but even more, you have responsibilities and they all weigh on your shoulders: your employees, your family's wellbeing, and your health, sanity, and—why not—your happiness.

The day-to-day grinding, the ups and downs of the business sometimes feel endless, sometimes feel overwhelming. Feelings like fear, lack of clarity and vision, frustration, being tired all the time, anger outbursts, and maybe a glimpse of depression are daily companions. Loneliness creeps up at times … and you have wondered if this is all that there is to it or if this is even worth it.

You *want* to make it worth it, you have invested so much time, energy, and money!

You know in your gut that you *need* to do something about it, you need to *be the person* who will make your business succeed, and you need to *become* the person who will not only love your business again but who will wake up excited every day to finally, once and for all, make your business go to the next level.

You are a warrior, a gladiator in the midst of the so many parts that make the machinery of any kind of business: people, product, systems, finances, legal, innovation … you are at the center of the action, you are *the* manager of them all, the one who oversees it and the one who everyone holds accountable.

This book is for the warrior who has fought many or a few battles, to the one who has won and lost a few of them, and has battle scars to show. To you who are reading this book, no matter how wounded you may feel right now, you are a warrior at heart and you still have the burning desire and the need to move forward, to conquer, to win, to step up.

You know you have it in you; you summoned it when you decided to start your business. Maybe you have lost some of it in your battles, maybe you have just forgotten, but I can tell you, I can assure you, *you have everything within you* to have your business expand, to make your business reach the success levels that you dreamed of at the beginning of your journey.

My deep admiration to you. I salute you for giving it all you've got in your soul, for pouring your heart, tears, blood, and sweat into your business. For daring to stand up and be vulnerable to all judgement and criticism, for still standing and drawing your courage, determination, and will every single day to wake up and bring yourself to your business to face the day.

Every single day in your business arena you are a warrior.

So right now, you, in your wisdom and humility, decided to look outside of yourself for knowledge and tools that will help you add shine to what you already have, that will help you bring your company to another level, to the level you know you deserve, to the level you have worked so hard for so long.

You have come to realize that external abundance—call it "money" in the business world—comes from first from within. If you had not realized this you would not be reading a book about how to feel excited in your business every day, how to stay motivated, and, as a very tangible result, how to exponentially grow your business!

It is my privilege to help you in your journey, I have been there many times, experiencing the ups and down, the tears and the laughs, the judgement and the admiration, and I know that at the end of the day this road is a lonely one many times.

You need to learn how to make yourself the best trip companion to your own self, and then you will be unstoppable.

SEVEN STEPS TO GROW YOUR BUSINESS, FEEL EXCITED, AND STAY MOTIVATED

There is a world of difference between *one day* and *day one.*

This, my friend, is your *day one.* You made a decision, took action, and now are about to embark on the extraordinary journey of the Zen Business Warrior: to conquer One's Self and to accomplish anything you set your heart and mind to.

The following is a brief description of each of the seven steps that you and I will be focusing on over the next days. Each of the steps is designed to build on the previous one, that way at the end of the book you will not only have a very clear understanding of these life-changing concepts presented throughout the book but you will also have applied these to your particular life and work situation. Yes, this, is not the "just read book" this is a "hands-on book" *to do, to take action, and move forward.*

Let's begin.

Step 1—Clarity: Know What You Really Want

Without a clear address, the most sophisticated GPS won't take you anywhere. The same is true in your life and therefore in your business: define where you are in terms of what you want and how you feel, define where you want to be in terms of who you need to become to get there. And fill in the gap.

Step 2—Your Reason Why: Why Do You Want What You Want?

Without a compelling reason *why you want what you want*, it is nearly impossible to summon and *sustain* the will and determination to make whatever you desire become a reality. *Making your business succeed does not have to feel so hard.* It will actually come with ease if you can maintain a clear focus in your mind and especially in your heart, and if every day you practice the feeling of what you want and anchor it with your why.

Step 3—How Will You Get It?

Without a solid and clear strategy, vision and a passionate desire can fall short. I believe you can find a way, no matter how, when you have an intense and clear desire. But I also believe that there is no need to re-invent the wheel. I love this Tony Robbins's saying: "Success leaves clues." Why not shorten the time it takes by learning from proven strategies? Strategies that have worked for me and for million others, which are now accessible to you in this book. This is what the book you are holding is about: the how to do it.

Step 4—Understanding What Prevents You: What Is Slowing You Down?

It is not enough that you know what you want and how to get it. *You need to take action.* A lot of people know what they are supposed to be doing, yet they don't do it. Why? What stops them? *What has stopped you?*

Here you will find out what your deep ingrained core beliefs are that have stopped or slowed you down from getting where you want to be. You will also learn to enhance those beliefs that have served you well. You will find out how paving the way for a peak emotional state every day can transform your business and your life.

I guarantee you that.

Step 5—Success: How Will You Know You Have Succeeded?

You will make your own markers—what success means to you. They will be your lighthouse in the dark times and your inspiration in the good times.

Step 6—Action: One Day vs. Day One

I can't emphasize enough how important taking action is. Most of the time baby steps, sometimes quantum leaps, sometimes you will "*stop, correct, and continue.*" It is all okay, as long as you keep moving forward.

If you allow me, I will be your personal coach throughout this book.

What do coaches do? Well, first they care about you. Not everything in this book may be new to you. Maybe I am reminding you of something you already know and will help to make it part of you. What do I mean? Simple. I believe you don't really "know" something when you understand it, when you've heard about it, or when you have read about it.

You only know something when you become it, when you live it.

I am here to help you every step of the way.

Step 7—Trust and Faith: Listen to Your Heart

Faith is when you expect something to happen with certainty because you have complete trust in yourself, trust in the Universe, trust in the cooperating components of your life creation, and, most especially, trust the knowledge that you are never alone.

WHO THE HECK IS LINA AND HOW CAN THIS BOOK HELP YOU?

First and foremost, I am an entrepreneur, just like you are.

A hardworking, smart, determined one like I am sure you are (otherwise you would not be reading this book). So let's do it by the book: I have a BS in business administration with a major in marketing, an MBA, and certifications that look all very nice on my office wall.

I have ten years of experience as a successful executive in leading corporations and for the past fifteen years I have been a business owner, an entrepreneur in one of the most competitive, cutthroat industries of our fast-paced world: telecommunications and technologies.

But, what I would really like to share goes beyond that: *I love my life*!!! And I want for you to be able to feel and say the same thing, on your own terms, fully living a magnificent life with those you love the way you want to. Life on your terms, freedom on your terms, deliberate and masterful creation of what you want and dream.

My goal with this book is to stir you up, inspire you, and give you the knowledge and the tools to take immediate deliberate control of how you are creating your life. To help you enjoy the ups and downs of your company and, most importantly, to enjoy your life while you are in the day-to-day grinding.

I would like every person that reads this book to feel inspired and directed to action, actions that are not complex nor hard to take.

Complexity is the enemy of execution. That is why this book is written in a sequence that will allow you to understand first with your mind, then with your powerful heart, and will allow you to take action by following my *Seven Steps to Grow Your Business, Feel Excited, and Stay Motivated.*

Yes, I will say it again in other terms: you will transform your life beyond your wildest dreams if you follow these steps. Hopefully your mind is churning now, hopefully you are having some excitement. And you may have some doubts too, that is perfectly fine at this moment.

I will only ask you to open your mind and just think of the following words every time you find yourself in a skeptic moment: *"What if what I just read is really how things are? What if I have been looking at the same thing in a very different way my whole life? Would this new perspective make a difference in my life?*

That is a powerful, powerful way to contemplate something new. It opens your mind, it tells your brain "okay, just go with it for the meantime." By doing this, you will allow yourself to have a different perspective than the one you are now experiencing, what you call your reality.

The most dangerous words a person can say are *"I know that."* These three words stop growth, stop expansion, stop interaction, stop new ideas from flowing, stop innovation. Pretty soon these words will make you obsolete in all aspects of your life.

Besides, we don't really "know something" just because we heard it at a great seminar, we read it in an amazing book, or we learned the concepts at a university. We only really know something when we live it, when we have become it, when it is part of our ingrained beliefs, which in turn have everything to do with how we view the world around us.

Our beliefs are the glasses through which we experience the world— mostly in automatic pilot, *until you decide* to pause and really take a look to see what part of that automatic pilot has served you well and what part has not.

HOW TO GET THE MOST OUT OF THIS BOOK: BECOMING THE MASTER

This book will walk you through my Seven Steps. It will take you through a journey comprised of the three levels designed to give you mastery.

And mastery means going deep. Like I said before, *you don't know it until you become it*, until you have mastered it. So let's review the levels. They are a guide to your map. This is how the Steps are meant to be taken or live out in your real, day-to-day life.

THE THREE LEVELS OF MASTERY

1. *Cognitive understanding* is your ability to understand a concept. Any person who reads or hears a concept can get it; it is only information. It is not rocket science. This is just the first step to pave your highway to the life you want. You may find yourself saying "I know this" or you may find yourself in an "aha moment" reading something put a certain way for the first time in your life and loving it. Still, this is just your first step and it is where 95 percent of the people stay.

2. *Emotional mastery.* Here is where the magic begins. In this step you will arouse your emotions, your deep-seated feelings about what you want and what you definitely don't want in your life— your desires, hungers, fears, concerns. When you are exposed to the information, to the concepts, with enough repetitions,

you will feel stimulated to ask, to experiment, to try, to move forward, to act. Here is where you make the commitment to stick to anything new in your life—to form new habits, to do the work it requires. Still, New Year's Resolutions belong to this step, wanting something to really change, but most of the time, not making it part of your life.

3. *The ultimate mastery: the physical mastery.* That means you don't have to think about what you do, your actions are second nature, it has become part of you because you have developed it into a *habit. And the only way to get to a habit stage is through consistent repetition.* "Repetition is the mother of all skills" Tony Robbins constantly tells us. You can acquire any skill though repetition, even happiness and joy. There is such a thing that I like to call The Muscle of Happiness.

Now remember something all throughout this book: this is not a book, it's a blueprint. Each section is designed to help you evaluate exactly where you are in your emotional and life-fulfilling terms and will help you close the gap between where you are now and where you truly want to be.

This is a journey of a lifetime, but I invite you to start here. You will come to realize that you only need to take little steps, with consistent repetition, to have a quantum leap.

If you are with me, let the journey begin!

"Most people overestimate what they can do in one year and underestimate what they can do in ten years"
– Bill Gates

Chapter 1
MY STORY

MY PERFECT BUBBLE ... OR WAS IT?

I just stared at the phone. He said yes and I could not believe it. I was actually looking at the very high possibility of leaving my country and moving to the United States.

David, my husband, had, just in a few words, changed the course of our well-established lives and opened a new destiny for us. Okay, so it was not a done deal yet. At the time, I worked at the leading telecommunications company in my country and there was a job opening, what everyone was calling "the dream job of the year." Now that I had my husband's support to apply, I would still have to participate in the recruiting process for the most coveted position the company had ever seen since its opening six years prior, and be selected among all those individuals applying—but I knew I was going to be the one chosen. I had no doubt. My initial fear of participating was that I knew I was getting the job. And two months later, I did.

I had the perfect job—earning probably three times what a thirty-year-old was making in the market then—at a great company. I had built wonderful relationships with the people in the office that became some of my closest friends. I was healthy and vibrant and I had been married to a wonderful man for three years. I had my life figured out, I felt invincible, life was perfect!

I remember vividly when my friend next to my office had jokingly said to me, "That job opening description sounds like they are describing you. Every single requirement is just you. You should apply for it!" I remember telling him with a smile, "There is no way David will quit his job and follow me to Florida! Besides, I love it here."

A few hours later I was on the phone with David and I made a joke—a joke! "Would you like to live in Miami?" I said and he paused, and quietly responded, "Yes, I would." After my initial shock, I told him all about the new position and what it meant for him: quitting his job (he was a director at the largest insurance company in the market), leaving his family behind for the first time in his life, and having no friends, no relatives, no one that we knew close to us there.

Still, he said, "Yes, okay, let's do it."

For me that type of personal attachments was non-existent since I grew up in different parts of the world. My dad had been a successful expat employee in an American multinational company, and every five to seven years we would move countries. Changing countries was like changing neighborhoods to me. Also, my parents lived in Costa Rica at the time and I did not have childhood friends to leave behind since I had just returned to my country for the first time in my life five years prior, so I had no attachments really. No heaviness in my heart plus my eternal disposition for a new adventure marked my easy yes to this opportunity. The only person I needed to consider in this decision was practically packing up already.

I did not know it then, but that March 2002 marked the beginning of my journey.

With big hopes, an adventurous heart, and an excited and positive soul I arrived in sunny Miami. It was June, really hot and humid, long sunny days … I was happy.

I had been one of the founding employees at my company. I was among the first twenty employees who, with just a business plan under our arms and a lot of determination, in a short period of ten months had a full telco company up and running with major economic groups as our parent holdings. No expense was spared; it was a fantastic playground! I had been working for five years when I applied to this dream position in Florida to lead the organization to penetrate the second largest target market in the world for our company.

I had changed to a new division, I had a new boss.

After I was appointed to my new position I stayed for another two months finishing the business plan and logistics before moving. I had only spent one week working with my new boss and I just had this guttural, un-resting feeling that it was going to be a challenge to work with him.

And it was. We never got along. I did not like working with him and he did not like working with me. It was like water and oil. Still, I thought, "Mmm … I will be in Florida and he will be here. I will call the shots there and I will make it happen—my way—and he will then let me be. Results will speak for themselves. This pit in my stomach is because I am just a bit anxious about all the changes at once, that's all."

I could not have been more wrong.

WHO PUSHED MY COW?

He was a genius, but in the "building relationships based on respect, trust, and loyalty" area? Not so much, in my personal experience. You know when people talk about emotional intelligence? Okay, he was a good example of all the "what not to do." I learned a lot from him, I promised myself I would never treat anyone that way, and thanks to that experience, today my company's philosophy is based on *"Delivering Happiness at Work,"* one that has fulfilled me and those who work with us in the most wonderful ways. *"Everything happens for a reason and it is always to our benefit."*

I had been an achiever all my life, an overachiever by any regular standard: straight A student, avid reader, well-travelled and cultured (thanks to my parents), bilingual, a jack of all trades when it came to sports, healthy and fit, and emotionally well-grounded thanks again in large part to a loving and nurturing childhood environment. I graduated with a bachelor's degree in business administration, had an MBA, and my career path took off really fast from the moment I submitted my first resume. I worked with two of the leading companies in their industries before I joined this one and pretty quickly I was doing amazing.

That is, until I took this offer and had this person to report to. Then all went down the drain.

Long hours at the office were a regular thing. Twelve or fourteen hours were the regular norm, but that was okay—it was a start-up and that was what I needed to do. The members of the Board had approved this project only if it was in the positives from the beginning, so the only way to do this was to keep all costs at a bare minimum. Before I left my country, my boss asked me to voluntarily sign a release to all my employee's rights if I wanted to take the position. It was made abundantly clear that if the project failed for any reason I had no rights to be relocated back to my country or transferred to another position or to have any kind of compensation for the years I had previously worked. I signed it all. In my mind, there was no going back and no room for failure—I had never failed before at anything related to my work, anyway.

Pressure to make the sales budget was there all the time, and that was okay too (I own and run a business—without sales, you don't exist!) but it was the way it was done, the feelings of being utterly alone with no resources to use (no marketing budget, no money for additional payroll, nothing additional) that made it extremely hard. I was working on all fronts at the same time. Once, I went with my husband to a Latin Food Fair. We both put on the company's shirt and cap and gave away 7,000 free sample cards to people coming in under a 95-degree Florida sun in summer for eight straight hours. We could not spare $200 for two students to do this!

When I called my old colleagues from other departments of the company to ask for help in areas that were not my expertise, like financial and accounting reports for the Board, I was told they had been told they could not help—that I had to do them myself. I never felt teamwork, or shared responsibility, or a guiding hand from him. This led to my just keeping it all to myself. I could not show any doubts or fear because it was just not acceptable. Anxiety, fear, self-doubt, and sickness crept into my world for the first time in my life.

In the course of fourteen months I shrunk little by little and became a shadow of that bright, happy, optimistic, smart, and resourceful person I had been. I felt emotionally battered with no compassion. It was an "all business, nothing personal, all for your own good" attitude, but at the end of the day I ended up a coffee and Redbull junkie and drinking any Guarana-infused tea I could find to keep me going—while at night taking sleeping pills to be able to disconnect for a few hours. I lost fifteen pounds, and I was already slim by any standard. I was skin and bones.

The problem: I was all alone, doing everything. It was a one-woman show and I had a business plan that just *had to* succeed no matter what.

If I did not, I was going to be out of a job, David out of a job, our lives upside down…

Then my deepest fear kicked in: my fear of failure. I never really cared much about money, about power, about approval—the "usual" drugs of choice. I liked them of course, but they were not what ruled my life. My fear of failure was my master and that particular component plus the hidden-agenda-kind-of-handling-matters my then-boss had with me was the perfect combination to make someone like me bend over backward to do everything, no matter if my sanity, my health, or my relationship with my husband was on the line. It all seemed secondary to me then.

The inevitable came to pass: I had a breakdown.

One regular day just before getting into my car I just crumbled to the floor and could not stop crying. I felt overwhelmed, could not breathe, I felt such physical pain in my chest I thought, "This is what a heart attack might feel like."

Some pills later I got to my feet and got to the office. I don't know how I mustered the will to do it, but I did.

It went on like this for a year. I can't even recall details now—those days are in a kind of a fog—I just remember the dreadful feeling of waving goodbye to David with a knot in my stomach and swallowing hard not cry, every single morning. He had his share, too. He had not been able to find a job for eleven months, and it was slowly eroding his natural optimism. At that moment he was the stronger of the two and held us together.

Everything happens for a reason and now I look back and I see that this time made him mentally stronger and also gave him the time to study real estate. Robert Kiyosaki (*Rich Dad, Poor Dad*) became our favorite mentor those days. This would become one of the stepping stones in my journey.

Just about two weeks before my first anniversary with the company, my boss travelled to Miami for a telco fair. I worked long hours for three days at the fair and at the end of the last day he just said, "We need to talk. This is not working."

Time stopped. My heart and soul sank. I felt like throwing up.

I had given my blood, tears, and sweat the past year, I had traded my life, I had uprooted David from his family, friends, and work. The business plan was doing perfect, we had become the leaders in the market segment we had targeted, it was a huge success, wiping out even the oldest competitor in the market. How could this be happening to me?

Two days later I was walking out, with my brown box and the shocked looks of my team. I clearly remember that day. That same afternoon I had an appointment with an immigration lawyer and he told me that I had thirty days to pack and leave—my working visa was expiring in two weeks. I felt like a complete failure. I felt a searing pain in my heart and soul like I had never experienced before. We went to Lincoln Road, a tourist area in Miami, and we both sat down in the middle of the pedestrian walk. The feeling was totally surreal: I had no job, my husband had no job, I had no working visa, in thirty days we would become illegal if we stayed, we had brought all our belongings from our country, including our two dogs. Resentment and rage never felt so real.

STORY—PUSHING THE COW OFF THE CLIFF
Original Author: Unknown
Rewritten by Philip Chircop

A long time ago, a Monk set out on his travels accompanied by his assistant, a Brother. Night was falling when the Monk told the Brother to go on ahead to find lodging. The Brother searched the deserted landscape until he found a humble shack, in the middle of nowhere. A poor family lived in the hovel. The mother, father and children were dressed in rags. The Brother asked if he and the Monk could spend the night in their dwelling. "You are most welcome to spend the night," said the father of the family. They prepared a simple meal consisting of fresh milk, cheese, and cream for the Brother and the Monk. The Brother felt moved by their poverty and even more by their simple generosity.

When they finished eating, the Monk asked them how they managed to survive in such a poor place, so far away from the nearest neighbors and town. The wife looked to her husband to answer. In a resigned tone of voice, he told them how they managed to survive. 'We have one cow. We sell her milk to our neighbors who do not live too far away. We hold back enough for our needs and to make some cheese and cream-that is what we eat."

The next morning, the Brother and the Monk said their good-byes and set out to continue their journey. After the Monk and the Brother had walked a few miles, the Monk turned to the Brother and said, "Go back and push the cow off the cliff!" "Father," the Brother replied, "they live off the cow. Without her, they will have nothing." The Monk repeated his order "go back and kill the cow."

With a heavy heart, the Brother returned to the hovel. He worried about the future of the family because he knew they depended on the cow to survive. His vow of obedience bound him to follow the orders of the wise Monk. He pushed the cow off the cliff.

Years later, the young Brother became a Monk. One day he found himself on the same road where he found lodging so many years ago. Driven by a sense of remorse he decided to visit the family. He rounded the curve in the road and to his surprise, he *saw a splendid mansion, surrounded by landscaped gardens, in the place where the hovel used to be. The new house exuded a sense of prosperity and happiness. The Monk knocked on the door.*

A well-dressed man answered. The Monk asked, "what ever became of the family who used to live here? Did they sell the property to you?" The man looked surprised and said he and his family had always lived on the property. The Monk told him how he had stayed in a hovel on the same spot, with his master the old Monk. 'What happened to the family that lived here?" he asked.

The man invited the Monk to stay with him as his guest. While they ate, the host explained how the family's fortune changed. "You know Father, we used to have a cow. She kept us alive. We didn't own anything else. One day she fell down the cliff and died. To survive, we had to start doing other things, develop skills we did not even know we had. We were forced to come up with new ways of doing things. It was the best thing that ever happened to us! We are now much better off than before."

FROM "WHY DID THIS HAPPEN TO ME?" TO "WHAT DID IT HAPPEN FOR?"

I now know that all that happened was the best that could have ever happened. All those long days and nights working my butt off, alone with everything on my shoulders, taught me everything I needed to know to start my own business. David had no job, so for twelve months he was my unpaid assistant. He helped me a lot, particularly with a new and revolutionary product that later became the basis for our own business.

When I said my goodbyes and thank-yous to all my distributors and providers, they expressed disbelief at my being fired and admiration for my work done in past months. That truly felt like a balm to me. My feelings of failure and embarrassment were crushing me, and to be asked by a couple of them on the spot if I wanted to work for them was marvelous medicine to my badly hurt ego.

I was hired two weeks later by an online start-up company back then when Yahoo and Terra were dominating the scene. David and I had made a pact: I would bring the daily bread and he would build our future.

He started our telco company, Alo Global Technologies, with no money, working alone from home. I would be there for our "board meetings" but he gave it his 1000 percent and shortly it began to payoff. A lot of hard work, a lot of dreams, always improving a little here and little there, always with the customers at the center of everything we did. They felt like family, more than customers. David knew them all by name and their stories since he would personally talk to them when they needed anything. He was a one-man show for anything that had to do with sales and customer service and support and everything else he outsourced to vendors. That is how our company, Alo Global Technologies, started. He poured his heart into it and I was always behind the scenes.

For the next eight years it steadily grew. I quit my job after two years and joined him. And little by little the company took form and we transformed it into a B2B telecommunication provider of some very innovative products in the Latin-American market. We worked hard, we were excited, optimistic, and it was gaining momentum. Our business flourished, our family too! We now had our children, Tamara and Daniel, in our lives. We felt blessed and contented.

Sometime parallel to the story of the beginnings of our company, the *Rich Dad and Poor Dad* phase arrived in our lives and we had the goal that we were going to have thirty properties in ten years for passive income. Years 1 and 2 went fantastically well. We acquired four properties and were really getting the hang of it.

It was the perfect idea, but the wrong timing: 2008.

The market crashed and with it, we lost our properties. It was a below-the-belt-blow, again. All the hard work, so many times while our friends were at the beach having a good day we were fixing walls and cleaning toilets, all the money we had saved over the past ten years, gone. Our home, gone.

Our safety net was our company. It was doing well, enough to give us a decent living, yet it was not "real money," not the one of our dreams. We were operating, but there is a huge difference between being a business owner and a business operator.

> *"Insanity: doing the same thing over and over again*
> *and expecting different results."*
> **– Albert Einstein**

2009, *THE* YEAR

It was 2009, and when I look back I can see the "coincidences," the serendipity of it all.

How things aligned back then. In the middle of our "just okay" business and losing our properties I began to ask myself: "*Is this all there is? Is this what I want? Is this enough? Really?*"

A book landed on my lap, a great book called *The Passion Test* by Janet Attwood, and that book led me to another one: *The Secrets of the Millionaire Mind* by T. Harv Eker. Two months later I ended up attending a free three-day life changing seminar they offered. At the end of the seminar, they presented me with a package for $20,000 for both my husband and I to engage with them in a two-year journey. The package was twelve seminars/camps on the West Coast, and I lived in Florida!

$20,000?!? WTF! Where would I get this kind of money? Plus plane tickets, accommodations, food, rental car … I had lost everything, where and how could I make this happen? I had two small children, two and four years old, and no rich uncle I could ask for a loan from. Our business needed us in the day-to-day to operate—how could we travel together every four months to the West Coast?

"YOUR LIFE CAN CHANGE IN THREE SECONDS." THIS IS WHAT THEY MEAN

I remember the exact moment my life changed, vividly: we were having lunch at a hole-in-the-wall Chinese restaurant, the food was getting cold on the table, David and I both stared at each other, each wanting to move forward, each paralyzed by "the hows." We had to make a decision right after lunch to get the "seminar discount" (yeap, we fell into that too, it works). I remember my heart was in my throat, my mouth was dry, and my hands were shaking. Yet somehow, I knew we could make it happen. We were smart enough and we were more scared of what would happen if we did not do it. That was the plain truth.

So, we bought the $20,000 two-year seminar package. The no-going-back-*huge*-decision was made.

Once again we had set sail into the unknown.

I remember my hand sweating and shaking when I was signing the paperwork. I only had $8,000 of available credit in my credit card. I had to find a way to get other credit cards or a loan to pay the rest.

I did. I found the way. That is why I really believe to the core of my being that when I made the decision and took the first step, all the forces of the Infinite and Powerful Universe stepped in and helped me with all the "hows."

I was able to get free airplane tickets, I was able to find deeply discounted hotel prices, I was able to find a way to have a family member come to my aid with my small children while I was away. One time both David and I left for twenty-one days, to do three seminars/camps back to back—it was the only way to save on airfare tickets. I knew that no matter the feelings of heart break and guilt I had over leaving my small children with my mother-in-law for twenty-one days, I was doing it to become a better person, a bigger version of myself, and in that process a better mom too.

How right was I! Those days were *the turning point* in our personal and professional growth journey and the beginning of an amazing economic abundance in our company.

Every time I get to tell our story, I love to show our employees our company's historic sales chart, because is the closest proof I have over my deeply ingrained belief that *"All growth comes first from within"* and that *"I create and attract to my life not what I want but who I am."*

The quality of my financial life, my emotional life, my health, and all the relationships in my current life are just the mirror of who I am right now. And it is always changing, something you have to work on, to nurture consciously. It is not like a diploma that you earned once and you can just hang on your wall.

Sales figures have been deleted for business confidentiality reasons.

On the previous page is the graphic of our company's sales over the past twelve years, where the increase of 500 percent in sales over the span of two years is absolutely clear—right after we made the decision to grow, to learn, to become more, to step out of the comfort zone.

I cannot graph my happiness, my health, or my emotional life the same way, so it may seem a bit shallow to show this but that is just the reflection that all growth comes from within first. Money is not the exception.

It was not overnight, it was not comfortable many times, it was not easy sometimes. Many times the "downs" hit me and it was really the time to show myself what I was made of—yes, there were plenty of those instances but one thing remained: my willingness to move forward in spite of fear.

I really believe that is key: you will always fear the unknown but if you only take the first step and trust with positive expectation then it will all be good.

I love this definition: "Expectation = Desire + Certainty."

I love to feel positive expectation. It does not bother me when things don't show up the way I wanted them to show up. I always believe there is a higher power at work and that sometimes my way is not necessarily the best way for me in the big picture.

I love to believe that *"Everything happens for a reason and that reason is to benefit me."* Believe, have faith, expect the best, always.

Don't be afraid of disappointments, don't put your bar low so you can reach it, don't play small, if you have a choice (and you have it—you have 100 percent free will to choose your thoughts) do not choose small. Always ask and expect to be blown away, and it will be so.

OKAY, LET'S PUT ALL THAT PERSONAL GROWTH TO THE TEST (SHE UP THERE MUST BE KIDDING ME!)

Then, another hurricane-force storm hit. Well, not really, this was more like a gradual thing, over the span of two years....

We had big plans. We went for it with no fear. No playing small was in our minds.

We tripled our payroll, we expanded our portfolio, we opened new divisions, we made the alliances, we had a brilliant business plan that considered all fronts. We had read, studied, and graduated from the one of the best business coaches in the world, Anthony Robbins Business Mastery (I love Tony, he really is the best. Marc Benniof says Salesforce, his 8-billion-dollar sales company, would not exist without the guiding principles taught to him by Tony. I feel the same about our business.) Both my husband and I have MBAs and years of experience in leading corporations and in our own under our belts, so we were ready to take it to another level.

Then, our sales started plummeting.

The first year was little by little, always justified: *"this is the normal learning curve for new products," "our main market suffered a devaluation of 30%," "some people quit—they could not cope with moving out of their comfort zone," "we lost focus," "we were doing great when we were specialized, now we have three times the portfolio and are masters of none"* and on and on…. Every time we arrived at a different analysis of the situation, every time we would "correct and continue."

Every time we would work harder, try harder, but it just kept spiraling down. Then one year turned into two years, and soon we were losing money every single month. It was nerve-wracking, frustrating, overwhelming … and depressing me.

I started dragging my feet around. Getting up from bed to make myself work was barely accomplished, I did it just out of sheer responsibility and resenting every minute. I counted the hours until the day was over, then I would start again the following day. I had a permanent knot in my stomach and a permanent shortness of breath from the anxiety.

I did not find meaning in my work, I felt incredibly guilty with David for not being nearly there, I beat myself up constantly, I kept saying that I was being irresponsible, mediocre, ungrateful, a procrastinator, unsupportive, a below-par leader to my people. *"So the going gets a bit tough and I throw in the towel?"* I felt like a hypocrite. Why couldn't I "walk the talk"? Now I chose to crumble? I was scared, bored, I felt my life was wasting away sitting at a desk ten hours a day. What for? Yeah, I had to pay the bills and take care of my family, but was that all there was to it?

"BE STILL AND KNOW." LOOK INSIDE FIRST

I knew that changes needed to be made again.

But what now? All that was from the realm of the business world to do like strategic planning, re-structuring, and execution of "correct and continue" I have been doing. I was actually sick "of learning life lessons" (this is what you say when you have a big freaking mess of a problem).

I knew it was time to look inside again.

And I did it the best way I know how to. I went back to all my mentors, all my loved books, my YouTube sessions with many many masters, both spiritual and action-oriented, I booked for myself and David a life changing seminar with Tony Robbins (again!). I must have spent over $100,000 in personal growth seminars, coaching, webinars, books, and travel expenses in the past twelve years.

I was going to go and humbly accept that I needed to really go inside again and that is what I did.

THE QUALITY OF YOUR LIFE IS IN DIRECT PROPORTION TO THE QUALITY OF YOUR QUESTIONS

When my company was at its highest point, what was going on with me? How was I? What was I feeling? What was my state of mind and of emotions? What was I doing that I loved?

I asked these questions and I noticed that right at the beginning, during the first year of our company, there was a natural excitement: new business, new opportunities. I had dreams of making a lot of money, I felt good, happy, excited about the day, every new sale was fantastic.

Then a trend of operations set in and we just rolled okay for the next eight years. We had a philosophy of *"we just have to hit this particular target, anything on top is welcome"* and guess what? That is exactly what happened every year. No more, no less.

Intention is a powerful creating force.

Then in the second phase of our business, we went full on with our intellectual, emotional, and personal growth and we really took off. We were netting in one month what we used to in a whole year.

Then our third phase: expansion, okay … here is where it got tricky. We are getting closer to what I now know without a doubt was the reason our business almost disappeared.

We focused 100 percent on the problems.

I will say it again: We focused 100 percent on the problems.

What you focus on expands.

At first slowly then *exponentially*. It gains momentum.

And that is what happened in a nutshell.

By focusing on the problems, we completely forgot all the things that made us feel good before: our experiences one-on-one with our clients, the funny anecdotes we used to share among us, our camaraderie among our team members, the thrill of winning a new account no matter the size, the excitement about creating a customized solution, the pride of being in the market for fifteen years and having some of the leading companies as customers. We forgot to celebrate small winnings. We forgot to laugh more, to deepen the relationships with our new team members, to just take a break and feel good, to be in the present and really appreciate what we had. Small things, nothing fancy. Yet so important.

We focused on the "doing" and nothing at all on the "being" part of the business. What we call "problems" will always exist—it is how you handle them that really makes a difference. Do we talk about them as a situation to fix and move on quickly to give 100 percent of our attention to the solution? Or do we dwell on them? Dwell on who to blame?

When we focus on the problems and the feelings of anger, frustration, fear that come with them and we dwell there then something pivotal happens: we lose focus, we lose clarity.

And when this happens you are at the mercy of the winds: all external factors can and will cripple your vision, your passion, your resourcefulness, you will lose sight of your "reason why" and you will then suffer the effects: stress, demotivation, lack of energy, lack of enthusiasm, lack of passion … and like a virus it will begin to infect everything inside you and all around you, and the biggest problem is that since it is a gradual thing, you don't notice it until it might be too late.

When you focus so much on the problems then that is exactly what you become: a problem fixer, all day putting out fires! Is there money and joy in that equation? Of course not!

WHAT YOU FEEL IS PARAMOUNT TO THE WELL-BEING OF YOUR BUSINESS

What you feel will determine how you create your life. *What you feel will determine the actions that you will take and these will determine your outcome.*

Having this awakening insight, little by little I gained back my serenity, my center, my alignment. This would not be complete if I didn't acknowledge here that all that you have read has been done hand in hand with David, my husband. We both work in our company, and he could have been the one telling this story. He is the CEO of our company.

It has been my role in our beautiful and deep relationship to be the one asking the questions. He has followed and built on the answers that we both have arrived to.

When we both started focusing our attention on the things that felt good, inside and outside our business, we began to feel clear and pristine *clarity*.

This led to very important decisions and actions (some of them personally painful), but the determinant difference was that they were aligned with our purpose, with our desire to feel joy again, to truly enjoy the path. *"Happiness is in the journey, not in the destination."* I had never felt these words clearer in my soul.

I gained back my enthusiasm and excitement. I would wake up in the morning and feel that the day would not be long enough for all the things I wanted to do!

And guess what: yes, the business took off again.

The secret in this book: how to get there and sustain it.

Chapter 2
STEP 1–CLARITY
KNOW WHAT YOU REALLY WANT

"ASK AND YOU SHALL RECEIVE." BUT ASK INTELLIGENTLY

About five years ago my husband and I took my wonderful mother-in-law to Israel. It had been on her bucket list for a long time and finally we were taking her to the Holy Land. Upon our return we made a three-hour stop-over in Paris' Charles de Gaulle International Airport for our connecting flight.

She had dreamed about going to Paris all her life and now she was in Paris.

Ever since, we have bantered with her to no end about this anecdote, telling her that she had to be more specific about her dream for it to come true exactly how she wished it, which I guess was more along the lines of strolling down the Champs-Élysées, having croissants for breakfast at a sidewalk café, going up the Eiffel Tower, and perhaps just sitting by the Seine River sidewalk and watching people go by. But, she only asked to go to Paris—and she got it!

SETTING YOUR DESTINATION

Where are you going? What do you want? Out of life, that is.

Most people struggle with these seemingly obvious questions. If you finish this chapter and can answer these simple questions you will be ahead of 97 percent of the people around you.

The first, pivotal step of this Seven-Step process is Clarity.

This means that you are without a doubt 100 percent clear on what you want your life to be like.

There are not enough examples, parables, and stories to emphasize the importance of having a clear picture of where is it that you want to go.

Most people are very clear about the things and circumstances they don't like in their lives, much clearer than the actual picture of what they truly want in life. Contrast is powerful, very powerful, that way and it can serve you here to establish where you are going. There is not a better time in your life to have pristine and powerful clarity than when you live something you did not like.

Now browse mentally through some of those instances and then turn them around into positive things you want in your life. Example: maybe you were sick with XYZ, and now you want a healthy, vibrant, and full of vitality body.

This is what you now want in your life, this is your destination. The *hows* will come later, right now is just what you want.

Then list where you are going, what you want in all the main areas of your life:

- Your health
- Your emotional state

- Your intimate relationship
- Your friends
- Your finances
- Your way of having fun
- Your family

When you have a clear destination you will set the GPS of your life on course, you will turn it on. If you don't have clarity about where you are going and what you want, then the "don't wants" will take over in repeating cycles and you will just keep going around, like in a hamster wheel, getting nowhere, ending up exhausted and without energy to go on. If you don't have a vision and clarity about the destination you want to reach, you'll simply never get there.

When you have no clear idea about your direction, all your hard work throughout the day really is not adding much value, it is not really serving you. You will be busy for sure, but that does not mean it is getting you where you really want to go. When you are clear, you are directing all your focus and energy to activities that are actually adding up to accomplishing your dream.

Again, this is deceptively simple. Once you understand it, you'll see why this may be the biggest thing in your life that is holding you back from breaking through to your next level: the life you actually want.

Take a moment and ask yourself right now what you want and, in connection to this, ask: *where am I right now* (with total honesty; it is not the time to write something that makes you feel good, but how it really is) and *where do I want to go.* Forget about the "how will I get there," this is very important, just express where you are going, what you want your life to be like.

Your business life is a part of your personal life—it is the means to an end—so right now, write what you want your life to be like, how you imagine it to be, both personal and in business.

Where you want to go has to be really compelling to you, really vivid, it has to give you goosebumps and teary eyes every time you allow yourself to dream about it. That picture in your mind has to be clear, adorned of all the great good things and experiences you want to have. It has to be so strong that it will pull you to them, you will not need to push yourself every day to create it.

Some people are afraid to get themselves in this picture. They would rather not visualize big so that they don't get disappointed. They would rather live a small life and determine this future dream based on the "what is" of the now. You need to understand something right now: *whatever your circumstances are now has absolutely nothing to do with your circumstances in the future.*

Whatever you are facing now does not determine your future.

Life will give you what you ask for. Always. 100 percent of the time, without exception. You just need to train yourself to ask intelligently, to really mean and feel what you ask for, and to move forward and train yourself to keep your momentum forward. *It is deceptively simple.* It is the never-ending journey to become the master of your life, much more focused on your internal growth than the titanic physical actions you may be thinking about right now.

No matter how bad you think you have it, ask now what you want, without limit and without thinking *"What do I want my life to be like? What do I really want?"*

You have heard of visualization or visual boards. They are wonderful and powerful life-creating exercises. In my opinion and experience, they can create a bit of anxiety. They sound formal and somewhat "life serious."

Meaning: you sort of have to know where you are going and have it a bit figured out to feel you can actually do a visualization exercise and glue some of your dream pictures in a board. Try this instead: how about if you just begin by daydreaming?

Yes, as light as it sounds, this word is the same mental exercise as visualization, but by using this word instead, you allow yourself to dream and think of anything you want, and since you are "daydreaming" there is no self-judgement on what you are dreaming about. There is not that small, annoying voice that says, "*What are you talking about? That is simply impossible!*" So, allow yourself to daydream now, and write down all that you want to do, to have, and to become.

Write it and own it. Know that is your birthright to desire anything that you want to have, anything you want to do, anything you want to become. Believe it is possible. Don't look back, just look forward, *decide* right now and proclaim to the Universe what you want. And then, and only then, when you allow yourself to daydream without restrictions, when you are feeling good about what you want, then this is the time to go look for some dream pictures and display them where you can see them daily.

Take the first step, write the coordinates in your Life GPS, and press "Go." Start right now. This is how you change your life in three seconds, making the decision about what you want and taking consistent and determined action toward it. Little by little, but always, always moving forward.

A decision is not when you are pondering, when you are evaluating the pros and the cons, when you are contemplating, when you are wishing you could. To decide means to commit to your dream, first believing it is possible then declaring it. Say it now. Write it down now.

With this book I want to help you take the next steps in the direction of creating the life you want, to being the person who will take your business to the next level, and especially to learning how to enjoy the ups and downs of the day-to-day.

Yes, it is possible. I have been there several times in my life and I can now say: you will learn how to appreciate even the negative situations and feelings. When you harness the mental and emotional power to do that, there is nothing that can stop you. You can and you will take control of what is happening to you emotionally and what is happening in your business, and ultimately you will define the quality of your life.

LIFE ON YOUR TERMS, FREEDOM ON YOUR TERMS

You'll also be able to apply these Seven Steps in helping your family and your friends.

People will begin to feel there is "something" different about you. As you start raising your energy and applying these steps in a consistent way every day, you will see the results, and other people around you will too. Eventually, you will become an inspiration to them when these steps become part of you.

It is not titanic work. You will not be heavy lifting anything for mindless hours, but it will involve a total and massive mental focus on each step of the way with a compassionate awareness toward yourself, every time you find yourself in a "correct and continue" situation. With no harsh judgements, with love and knowing that every single day is a new day and that you are doing perfectly fine, that you are where you are supposed to be, that you are not alone and that Infinite Intelligence has your back.

A BUSINESS PERSPECTIVE ON WHAT YOU WANT YOUR LIFE TO BE

The Real Problem: Lack of Resources or Lack of Resourcefulness?

We make decisions every day in our businesses. As heads of our businesses, this is what we do: a constant juggling of resources to reach our goals. We deal with customers, with our employees, our providers, our cash flow, our product development, sales, marketing, systems, customer service, and many others, always trying to keep all balls in the air.

I remember that every time we had a bump in the road (or an abyss to cross!) I would stop and analyze what it was that we were doing wrong.

What component of all of the resources I was juggling was not aligned to the rest of the system? I spent countless hours with my husband David analyzing all the details of what was wrong and how to fix it. We have always worked under the philosophy of "correct and continue," just keep moving forward, do not let anything paralyze you. Paralysis by analysis has never been our problem. We welcome change and risk. We both have always been more concerned about the consequences if we did nothing.

During those days, I remember that at some point the problem was that we had "most of our eggs in the same basket" and we had turned too complaisant, too comfortable.

Right after we did all the courses I mentioned at the beginning of the book, we attracted (literally) one of the biggest customers, in terms of sales, our company has ever had. To this day we don't even know how they got here, I swear.

One day we received an email and someone was asking about our services—and we didn't do any heavy advertisement, never had. Just days later they became our client. It all just flowed in effortlessly.

With that client, our company grew exponentially for the next few years, not just in sales, but the margins were fantastic even after providing them with savings well over 40 percent compared to what they had! It was absolutely phenomenal. I recall this period of time as one of abundance, joy, and expectations of many greater things to come.

Then, we started worrying that 45 percent of our total sales were from one single customer and that we were really kind of taking it easy with our sales team while they were selling about 60 percent of their quota.

We came to the conclusion that we wanted to have a higher ticket sale, since that was one of the quickest ways to increase revenue, right? But we needed more sophisticated products to do that.

So we went head on and transformed our company: we tripled our payroll, we tripled our portfolio, we engaged in many alliances and closed amazing distribution deals with very innovative companies from the technology world. We also tripled our operating costs.

We developed a very clear and detailed road map. It all looked fantastic on paper. We had the ideas, we now had the products and the alliances, we had hired the right people, and we had the desire and determination to make it succeed.

But it went completely the other way. The implementation was not without flaws and we started to choke and very soon we were just drowning in problems. All types of problems: problems with our customers, with our employees (in two years we had an almost 100 percent rotation of our most qualified personnel) and especially huge problems with our new divisions. It was a constant putting out of fires, and it was emotionally overwhelming.

Frustration and anger were just on the surface for everyone, including us. Lack of motivation, lack of initiative, eroding determination, definitely lack of fun and passion marked those very dark days in our company. And like the saying goes, "When it rains, it pours."

THE PROBLEM WAS NEVER LACK OF RESOURCES; IT BECAME LACK OF RESOURCEFULNESS

And this only means that it is about your attitude. Your emotions that can make or break your business.

The problems were never all the things that I enumerated that eroded the company, it was what we as the leaders of our company focused on: we focused on the problems and we let our emotions of the moment dictate our actions, or rather reactions, from a place of fear, scarcity, anger, and frustration.

Usually business people, when facing a tough time, believe that it's from lack of knowledge, lack of time, lack of money, lack of technology, or lack of the right people. But the reality is that it is never about that. What it really amounts to at the end of the day is lack of creativity, lack of determination, lack of curiosity, lack of resolve and resilience, lack of love, and finally lack of passion.

What do they all have in common? They are all emotions. The right emotions can lift you and your team out of any situation. Any problem can be solved no matter how hard it looks at the moment.

The wrong emotions over a sustained period of time, on the other hand, are what make so many businesses fail.

When you define where you want to go in your life and in your business, *define it in terms of how you want to feel on a permanent basis.* Everything we do is because we want to feel better, more happy, more joyous, more free, more loved, more appreciated, more confident, more fulfilled, more proud of ourselves. It revolves around feelings at the end of the day.

Let me share a powerful exercise from Dan Sullivan on how to get total clarity with the help of your emotions. Imagine it's one year from today and when looking back over the past year, you realize that it was the best year of your life. What does that look to you? What would have to happen for you wake up every morning on fire, free of frustrations, and totally convinced you were not wasting your potential, wasting your life? Think about what the best year of your life would look like and get emotional, get engaged, get engulfed in your heart and soul expansion, fuel it, let your goosebumps and teary eyes free and fuel it even more. Visualize now specific details about what made it so amazing.

Ask yourself the following questions when you look back at this year:

- *How much money are you making? How much money have you saved away for your family's security? How does this make you feel?*
- *How is your business doing? Are you taking it to the next level? Are your employees happy? How excited do you feel every day?*
- *How is your relationship with your spouse or your partner? Do you feel connected and supported? Do you have an amazing emotional and sex life?*
- *How is your relationship with your kids? Are you their friend? Do you have fun together?*
- *What exactly does your life look like a year in the future when you look back and it was the best year ever of your life?*

If you have not done so yet, write it down, just let it flow, don't go halfway. Get out of your head and do it from your heart. You see, when you know where you are right at this moment, you possess a true starting point. Then, when you take the time to look backward from the future in order to decide where you want to go over the next year, you have done more than most people who are stuck in one place. They ignore this simple habit and process for really establishing their direction, setting their Life GPS coordinates.

You know who does not ignore it? Successful people.

When you know where you are going you start being very, very conscious of many things that were just in automatic before. You start being the gatekeeper to your desired life and you start filtering certain things, like saying no to people who have been toxic in your life and business, saying no to certain obligations, saying no to certain business proposals, saying no to certain lifestyles that don't serve you well, saying no to unhealthy food, saying no to certain emails, or even choosing very carefully what you read and watch every day.

When you do this exercise you stop feeling overwhelmed, because only then will you determine how to spend your limited and most precious time and energy. You will not waste this on activities that have nothing to do with your dream.

Once you know where you are and you know where you want to go, you'll find it easier to acquire other success habits.

THE POWER OF CLARITY: RICHARD'S AMAZING STORY

Clarity is the most powerful manifestor there is. Pay attention to this story; it could be you in a few days.

One of my dearest friends is a man in his early fifties. Let's call him Richard.

Richard was a corporate man all his career life. He loved the structure of a well-organized corporation, loved the corporate lingo, loved the board meetings, loved the race to the top, and even loved the dress-for-success code in the financial industry. He worked for almost twenty years, was doing well, and always provided for his family. Then one day there was a restructure in the company and they closed his division. He was out of a job and he decided to go into his own business and be his own boss.

It all started well. The excitement of the new and fresh dreams pushed him forward, for a while. A couple of years went by and the dreams lost their shine.

Deciding to look deeper into himself as to why he just did not feel excited anymore, he took a very powerful clarity test called *The Passion Test* by Janet Attwood. He then wrote down that he wanted a job in a world top leading finance corporation, he wanted X amount as a salary, he wanted to travel for business, he wanted to enjoy all the perks of the corporate world, including the dress code, and that on top of that, he wanted to have this company to be somehow related to Brazil because learning and speaking Portuguese as his third language was a passion that he had always immensely enjoyed.

Guess what happened? Yeap, you got it right.

Less than thirty days later he got it all by a series of "coincidences." Yes, all that he asked for and wrote in his journal. When he told us about this, we could not believe it! And then again, that is the power of clarity and intention in your life. I have seen it happen in our lives, I saw it happen in his life, and I've seen it happen in so many stories of our employees, clients, and close family members.

I am here to help you every step of the way, to be your accountability partner, but at the end of the day it is your choices that determine your life. Be very clear about what you want in life and declare it aloud, summon it to you first and then act upon it.

Choose well, my friend.

NEED ANOTHER BUSINESS REASON
TO DEFINE WHERE YOU ARE GOING?

"80% of new businesses close before their 5th year and only 4% still remain by their 10th year." (Still exist—not necessarily thriving.)

You may have heard a market statistic like this at one point or another. Some of us might find it an exciting challenge (*"I will be part of this elite and smart 4% group that makes it!"*). Some of us might instead fill with dread and look the other way in avoidance and think, *"This will not happen to me."*

There is an immense array of methodologies and concepts on how to build, run, and develop a successful business. The access to information is now immediate. We live in the era of information and we are inundated by it. The problem now is not lack of knowledge.

A couple of decades ago the famous saying was *"Knowledge is power."* Yes, it was, because its access was limited to a few. You now know it is not so anymore. You can, at any given moment, just google something, go to your closest library, take the best-sounding marketing or sales or process online optimization course you can find, instantly, anything is just a click away

You may even be thinking *"maybe the real problem is where to turn, which one to choose, which would work best for me and my business."* It is a jungle out there, and it can feel overwhelming. It can also feel like you are being left behind since it is so hard to keep pace with the sickening speed everything seems to be happening at now (and to have a life, that is).Or you may even have experienced FOMO, the Fear of Missing Out on an opportunity or a good experience, which now contributes to increasing levels of anxiety and psychological dependence associated with the advent of the Internet and our modern world.

Knowledge is not power, actionable knowledge is power. Execution is power.

What does this mean? That no matter how much you understand something, no matter how much you want it, at the very end of the day what is important is that you do what it takes to make it happen.

And I will tell you something right here: it is not titanic work, it is not hard numbing physical type of work, it does not involve extreme sacrifices, it has nothing to do with a *"No pain, no gain"* type of mentality (though this works perfectly at the gym when you are pumping iron*)*.

Tony Robbins states that the chokehold on the growth of the business is always the leader. He is well known for this formula:

Success = 80% Psychology + 20% Skills

Your psychology, as a business owner, is the key that turns on your engine to execute, to create, to accomplish. You are the key.

You may learn the best skills in the world (heck, you may even have them) but if you don't execute due to your emotional set point, it amounts to nothing.

How you view and give meaning to all the things, events, and circumstances of your day-to-day life is what determines how you feel, whether you are excited and enthusiastic or you are indifferent and frustrated.

And how you feel determines not only what you will do but for how long you will be able to keep executing until you reach your goals.

Your psychology is the driving force that creates an extraordinary business and a magnificent life … or not.

So when you have clarity about where you are going and why you want it, this clarity gives way to action, inspired action. This means you will push through obstacles that are normal to have in a day-to-day business operation. But since you know where you are going and you have it anchored in your heart, you will become very resourceful and will make it happen no matter what. You will find the way. It is the psychology part of you that makes the difference—skills get you there faster.

That is the power of clarity in your life.

Chapter 3

STEP 2—YOUR REASON WHY WHY DO YOU WANT WHAT YOU WANT?

INSPIRATION AT 30,000 MILES OF ALTITUDE

Ten years ago at 30,000 miles of altitude in an American Airlines flight, inspiration hit us.

David and I were flying back home from Los Angeles after attending a fantastic five-day seminar (part of the package we had committed ourselves to that I mentioned earlier).

We had been working non-stop since we boarded the plane. We had just come out of one of the best marketing intensive seminars I have ever attended and we were completing the details of our company's marketing plan; we were breaking it down to a road map for us and our team. We were on fire for four hours! Then we finished and looked at all the activities for the next months, and it felt overwhelming to say the least!

We stopped and asked ourselves: *why are we doing all these trillion things?* We really needed a strong reason "why" to keep us going, for it to pull us toward it instead of us doing all the pushing with a sheer and titanic willpower. We were a small company, after all! I mean, you can push yourself all you want, but it is just not sustainable in the long run.

When our answers came back about "making our business succeed," "making a ton of money," "financial freedom," "delivering fantastic value to our customers," "providing for our loved ones" among others, they sort of fell kind of short. Don't get me wrong, we wanted all of that and more, but the question was: *what for?*

We ended up concluding that all that we ever wanted was to be happy, to feel good, to feel joy and appreciation, and the success, the money, were just a means to an end, so what was the end?

In the attainment of anything, all we ever want at the end of the day is to be happy—as a person, as part of a family, as part of a community— and to be able to facilitate that to those we love.

This happiness takes different forms for each person and it is in the finding of the particular form that one can spend a lifetime trying to find happiness, just to realize at the end that you don't find it, that it has been within you all the time.

So, as I was saying, when we realized the amount of time and effort it would take us to do all we were planning to, we said, *"Why don't we start by being happy at work, since we spend at least eight hours there every day? We really don't have to wait until the end of the day, weekend, or vacations when we are with our family and friends."*

"Delivering Happiness at Work in ALO" was born right there, that is, in our company ALO Global Technologies. We found inspiration in the Zappos story, a wonderful case of what focusing on happiness can do to a company in terms of growth and contribution.

Delivering Happiness at Work in ALO has been our company's Culture Philosophy ever since that day. We developed a complete program with its own identity for our *Familia ALO,* with company values, a logo, slogan, Joycom (our own mascot speaker, a very witty chimpanzee), our in-house newsletter, Familia ALO Retreats once a year where 100 percent of our employees are invited to a nature-surrounded destination for three days dedicated to personal growth and fun (we have done rafting, waterfall rappelling, caves, horseback riding, hiking, paintball, obstacle courses on water, among many others).

These retreats are the highlight of the year and are cherished by everyone. We always invite top notch personal growth coaches and David and I also actively participate, delivering all the knowledge and insights we have gained in our seminars and life experiences. We have made the saying *"Happiness is the journey, not the destination"* our mantra in our business, the words "enjoy what you do" are always there, quick to be re-called in many instances.

I believe this has been our strong rock to hold onto whenever we've been hit with hurricane-5-force circumstances. In times of challenges, we bring all this to the particular situation we are facing and remember the reasons why, the fun moments, our wonderful people, and whatever is happening seems like the edges lose their sharpness and we get to slow down, breathe deep, and change the perspective. "Nothing really is as bad as it seems" is about detaching yourself a bit, looking for that aligned center, and then just doing what you've got to do, but always, always let your actions and decisions come from your aligned center first.

We decided to build this Happiness Culture in our business because we were looking for a strong reason why, one that would transcend us, one that would be bigger than us as individuals. We set out for this and we got so much more! Yes, we have given a lot—our time, our energy and money to do all this—but the truth is that we have received benefits back tenfold.

Granted, not all has been perfect. I am talking here about a place where emotions are involved. Yes, of course I am talking about Happiness—what could be more emotional than that? It goes hand in hand with Love and Gratitude feelings that we openly discuss and immerse ourselves in when we go to our annual retreat. Dealing with individuals, with their beliefs, expectations, fears, and dreams; dealing with personal relationships in a business environment that is designed to produce income (we are not a charity foundation) is not an easy task.

When you input a component such as Delivering Happiness, it can become a double-edged sword: we really have to live what we preach every single day. Our values hold us accountable. Every single employee expects things from us and we expect things from them. We have three personal goals for everyone in this order of importance: personal growth, professional growth, and economic growth. This is our promise to each person we hire.

When you put your personal feelings on the line, you put yourself in a vulnerable place. I've had big disappointments, huge, with individuals that came on board in the very beginning and shoulder-to-shoulder helped us build the company. People that I grew to appreciate and love. And in a couple of circumstances I had my trust broken and my feelings battered … my soul mourned when we had to let them go or when they chose to leave. It was never about performance, the company's or theirs. It was issues related to our human nature: feelings, perceptions, expectations not met by either side.

But you know what? I will choose the risk of living a few instances of pain and deep disappointment in my life if this was the cost of having the wonderful, deep relationships we have built with our team over the years. These relationships and the way we work fill our souls with purpose and fulfillment. It makes us feel we are contributing, that we are positively impacting their lives and the lives of their families; in short, we are helping make a better world in our circle of influence, and it feels really good!

It is our goal to have a successful company, one that delivers extraordinary services and simply *wows* our customers. We cannot expect to deliver this in a consistent way if our employees don't feel the same within them first. When you read "go the extra mile," it goes both ways. Both sides must have something personal at stake.

"It is only business." My very personal take on this: this is the excuse that a person uses to be able to think, say, and do things that otherwise would not be acceptable. This short phrase excuses inexcusable behaviors, those without collaboration and compassion present in their business lives. I don't believe one who lives by this type of philosophy can actually find happiness and fulfillment in their life.

Don't get me wrong: if I need to fire someone because they are not delivering results, I definitely do. If I need to change to a new vendor because of better conditions that will benefit my business, I will. It is the way things are done, when you speak and do from your heart, with calmness, clarity, and the truth, you can do and say anything you need to.

And you will always be at peace, your integrity whole, and you will feel you *"walk the talk"* and can look anyone straight in the eyes, because you can look at yourself in the mirror.

A strong personal *reason why* for your business will be your strongest mental and emotional asset in your life. It will inspire you when you feel down, it will make "the fight worth it" when you feel you are at your wit's end, and the instances when you actually bring to life your "reasons why" (for example, us seeing how the lives of our team were impacted and uplifted during so many of our Encuentro Familia ALO over the years) will bring to you a feeling of immense fulfillment and purpose.

"Success without fulfillment is the ultimate failure."
– Tony Robbins

UNDERSTANDING WITH THE HEART: WHO AM I?

The question of the sages of all times. The question that all philosophers and religious figures have answered over the centuries, many very different from each other, some with common denominators.

I can just give you my take from my perspective, my experience, and my interpretations of so many masters I've had the privilege to hear, to read, to ponder, and that now I own by living it.

Every day I do my very best to act according to what I know to be the truth that empowers me and the days I don't, I have learned to not beat myself up, to just go easy on myself and accept with love that I am in my Life's Journey and that it is how I live that journey that really matters.

I also have come to fully understand at a mental, emotional, and spiritual level that the most important relationship I will ever have in my life is with myself, that there is nothing I can give to others that I don't have within me first, and that I don't give myself first, call it love, compassion, patience, appreciation. And that when you give it to others without really feeling it for yourself first (for example: love, appreciation, patience) then an imbalance occurs and at some point you will feel the emptiness of the imbalance.

I love my life! I am truly grateful for all the events and circumstances, all the good and the not so good, that have led me where I am now: a place of appreciation, gratitude, fulfillment, and personal purpose.

When you are in a place of present appreciation for who you already are and for your current conditions, and you feel positive expectations for all the new and good to come, you are in the best place you can be: one of peace and serenity yet excitement, and inspired to take action.

Your true power, your absolute power, resides in the appreciation for your magnificent self, to fully embrace who you really are, to nurture it, to expand it every day.

And when you fall into the mistake of criticizing yourself, blaming yourself, or even feeling guilty about not doing something or maybe about making a mistake, just stop for a moment, breathe, and know that is a part of you sabotaging yourself. There is nothing, absolutely nothing, more detrimental to you and to the success you work so hard for than to deprecate yourself.

Take it easy. Really. Just take it easier on yourself, correct what needs to be corrected, and continue. Leave behind all negative emotions toward yourself.

Be still and know, really know, that you are on the right path. If this book fell into your lap, you are on the right path, you are now on the path of finding the true heart of the Zen business warrior that is within you. It always has been, you just need to connect to it again. Soon you will come to see in your life all the things you want and you will feel an immense sense of peace, fulfillment, and gratitude.

WE ARE EMOTIONAL BEINGS—THAT IS WHO WE ARE

It is our emotions that rule and determine the choices we make, and these choices determine the quality of our life and our sense of purpose and fulfillment—or not.

But first, how do these emotions manifest—what triggers them? How do they arise in you? Most of time they come as an immediate reaction—that means that you really did not make the decision to respond, your subconscious did, and this automatic pilot is shaped by your beliefs, which in turn are shaped by your experiences.

Let's go deeper now:

Away from Pain vs. Toward Pleasure Actions
Which Makes You Tick More?

The force that shapes your life, the one that determines your emotions, is your primal response to pain and pleasure. Everything you do, everything I do, we both do either out of the need to avoid pain or our desire to gain pleasure.

So many people talk about the changes they want to make in their lives, yet they oftentimes do not follow through to the end result. What follows is an immense sense of frustration, overwhelm, and anger with themselves that finally arrives to guilt and self-deprecation, emotions that belittle and crush beyond words who we really are.

The problem is that people try to change a behavior, which in this case is the effect, instead of dealing with the cause behind it. When you understand the real reason behind your decisions, you will acquire immense clarity and insight on what needs to be done and why, and then, and only then, will you feel compelled to do it.

If you are making a decision in your business because you are afraid of an outcome (that is, to avoid pain), be very careful—usually this type of decision will in the end produce exactly what you were trying to avoid. If on the contrary, a business decision is taken because you want something to happen, it really excites you, you can imagine yourself in the outcome, and it makes you feel good, go for it. You may feel fear when you start pondering, "*how will I do it?*" or "*where will I get the money or resources from?*" But if your innermost feeling is one of excitement, like I said, go for it! Take the first step, set the ball in motion—it is about the momentum to make things happen.

Remember when I told the story of how, in the middle of my first financial crisis, after we lost our home and investments, I bought a $20,000 seminar package? Okay, I will admit, I was really looking forward to learning new things from masters (pleasure-oriented) but I was more scared of what would happen in my life If I did not do it (pain avoidance).

The decision in the moment was more based on pain avoidance (the fear of regret and unfulfilled potential), but sustaining the decision and taking actions for almost three years, actually making it happen, came from a burning desire to grow, from the exciting thought of great things to come, from the yearning to become more, no matter how uncomfortable everything looked at the beginning.

Identify Your Whys

So, finally, your moment of truth for this step.

Clarity is a powerful force, but what make it become a reality is your powerful "why."

Why do you want what you want? And this has to come from a deeper part of your heart and soul than knowing your destination. The issue here is that most people only scratch the surface here, they don't go deep enough. Most people will come up with an answer from the brain, the logical reason why. Things like: "I want more money to be financially independent," or "I want to lose weight to look good." They are good reasons, but they don't have the depth of purpose necessary for you to push through your most challenging times.

Here are some examples of your "why":

- *Why do you want your business to get to the next level?*
- *Why do you want your income to skyrocket from where it is?*
- *Why do you want to retire your parents?*
- *Why do you want to have more excitement in your business?*
- *Why do you want to have a deep and fun relationship with your spouse or partner?*
- *Why do you want to have a body filled with vitality?*

When you have a clear "why" from your heart you become unstoppable. Fear is the number one reason why people don't push through the finish line; fear is the brake that slows us down or stops us. But, a huge "but" here, when the reason why you want something is engraved in your heart and soul, you will find the way, no matter what. This fire does not get easily extinguished, like so many things we think we want.

This book is filled with steps, tips, golden nuggets of wisdom that will make you form new habits to push through your barriers, but the only things that can get between you and your dreams are the non-serving thoughts of your mind, and you can train your mind if your heart has a very clear, pristine, strong, emotionally-charged, and purposeful reason why.

The Seven Levels Deep Exercise

Some time ago, a speaker at a T. Harv Ecker Enlightened Warrior Camp took us through this incredible exercise to go really deep into our "reason why" and gain absolute clarity. I would like to share it here.

It is deceptively simple, yet powerfully deep. It consists of asking yourself seven times, "*Why do you want what you want?*"

Let me present an example to illustrate the exercise:

- Level 1 (general question): *What is important to you about becoming a successful real estate investor?*
  Response: *To make more money.*
- Level 2: *Why is it important for you to make more money?*
  Response: *To get out of debt.*
- Level 3: *Why is it important for you to get out of debt?*
  Response: *To stop working so hard to pay someone else.*
- Level 4: *Why is it important to you to stop working so hard?*
  Response: *Because I want to do things in my life with the fruits of my labor.*

- Level 5: *Why is it important for you to do things in your life…?*
  Response: *To take care of my mother who is widowed and needs help.*
- Level 6: *Why is it important for you to take care of your mother…?*
  Response: *Because she sacrificed everything to send me to college and I want to make sure she is taken care of in her golden years.*
- Level 7: *Why is it important for you to make sure she is taken care of…?*
  Response: *Because I want to be in control of my life so I can help those around me (who can't help themselves) know they are precious, worthy, and loved.*

In *Summary*, what is important to you about becoming a successful real estate investor?

The Big Reason WHY is: So you can be in control of your life and help those around you (who can't help themselves) know they are precious, worthy, and loved.

Now, my friend, it is your turn.

Let me help you with the first question: *Why* are you reading this book? I am reading this book because …

Then go seven levels deep and find pristine and powerful clarity like you have never had before.

THERE IS A BIT OF A PROBLEM, A BIT OF A CHALLENGE

The thing is that most of us place our focus in the short term, especially now in this too-fast-paced world. So whatever you think will create pain or pleasure in the short term is what you will most likely do, yet what we most value really is built in the long-term: relationships, health, purpose, joy, contribution. So you will need to really break through the barrier of the short-term pain in order to obtain the long-term pleasure.

The good news: you just need to be really clear about what you want and why you want it. This becomes your inspiring force that pushes your forward. It is here that your values and beliefs play a determinant role.

Remember too, that it is not *actual pain* that drives us, but our fear that something will *lead to pain*. And it's not *actual pleasure* that drives us, but our belief—our sense of certainty—that somehow taking a certain action *will lead to pleasure*. We're not driven by the reality, but by our perception of reality.

THE GRAYEST *TOLERATING* ZONE

I have a phrase (by now, you have read many of my Golden Nuggets phrases—they actually guide many of my decisions): *"You get in life what you tolerate."* This to me is the most difficult emotional situation to deal with, because there are so many things in personal and business life that you simply get used to. They don't feel dramatically bad … you grow to tolerate them. Even if you know they are not good in your life, you tend to look the other way and even justify them.

When you tolerate something, you don't feel good, you feel choked and angry. You have two choices: either you change the way you see them, shift your perspective, look for something good and totally and wholeheartedly accept it as it is, or just remove it from your life.

Either way, know that tolerating leads to a mediocre experience, not only because in that particular aspect you are tolerating you are settling for less than you know you deserve or are expecting, but what is even worse is that you are creating a habit to tolerate other things and justify by "I'll deal with it later—life is not perfect anyway." Know something: *life is perfect*, all of it, the good and the bad—all play a role. It is the glasses through which we see life that need to be cleaned or changed if they don't serve us, if they don't empower us, if they don't make us feel good.

Remember the fable about the frog being cooked alive in tepid water? She was cooked to death without realizing the temperature of the water was constantly increasing, and at a certain point it was too late. Too graphic an example? Life can hit you like that sometimes, if you let it.

These circumstances you tolerate in life need to be taken out by the root. You need to stop and really evaluate them—what are those circumstances or people that you are just tolerating in your life? If it is circumstances, they are much easier to address, but when it comes to people … well, that is more complex. Still, it needs to be taken care of.

Give it your best shot to improve it. Talk to them, be very clear about how you feel, what you would like to happen in order to continue with the relationship, define compromises, theirs *and* yours. Put a date on the calendar, review it then, and if nothing has improved, make the decision to stop tolerating it in your life.

This is a double-edged sword. I would strongly suggest that you be sure to come from a place of peace and of really wanting to improve whatever you are dealing with. If you don't, pretty soon you will use this phrase to remove everything that "does not bend to your wishes" and that you "will not tolerate anymore," and that is not the point here.

My invitation is for you to get in touch with your emotions. Since most people take action in order to avoid pain, realize that tolerating something is *the grayest part of our avoiding of pain.*

When you love something, *you know.* When you hate something, *it is clear to you.* What happens to the majority of stuff that happens in the *"tolerating zone"?*

A LESSON COURTESY OF THE GRAYEST TOLERATING ZONE

I mentioned earlier that a few of years ago we decided to expand our portfolio, to diversify, to increase the average sale ticket item by offering more sophisticated and innovative solutions. One of the first strategies in our business plan to be able to accomplish this was to bring onboard new talents.

We strongly believe that you can only grow as much as you have the right people onboard. Individuals that share the vision you have for your company, feel the thrill of making it happen with you and the team, and have the commitment and attitude to see it through. Notice that all I have just mentioned has more to do with the kind of person and not the technical skills, knowledge, and "certificates" they may bring too.

Anyway, getting into unchartered waters with these new divisions and services and being a bit anxious (translation to layman's terms: insecure and fearful) we decided to put more weight on resumes of individuals that came from companies that "*have been there and done that*" and on very impressive and well-written accomplishments on their resumes.

We hired a man with a very high profile and who had had a stellar career in a company ten times the size of ours. We believed he was going to help us put our company and our new sophisticated services on the map and beyond!

Intuition sucks sometimes. We "knew it" from the beginning that he was not a match. He did not really share our company values, did not value our Delivering Happiness at Work philosophy, and his attitude made it clear that he did not really care about taking the business to another level—even if his words were to the contrary.

I guess now he was there for an immediate short-term need, and that is okay—it was his choice of life then.

What was not okay at all was first, that we did not listen to that little voice that tells you something is off and but you can't quite pinpoint it.

We so much wanted to believe he was with us for the right reasons, that he was almost "Universe-sent," that we deceived ourselves into believing it was so.

We got into the terrible grayest of tolerating zones for almost a year! I can say now that within the first thirty days we knew he was not a good fit for us and that maybe we were not a good fit for him, either. But we let it drag on for twelve months! His lack of involvement, lack of commitment, "missing in action," busy-ness with "personal affairs," and crap excuses went on for a year!

What made us not fire him on the spot in so many instances? We tolerated all of this waiting for results that never came: zero, zip, zilch, nada, was ever accomplished.

It is actually a record in our company: the one person who has stayed the longest without producing anything. His fault? None. Ours? Absolutely 100 percent.

YOU GET IN LIFE WHAT YOU TOLERATE

What does tolerating something really mean? It means that you are compromising your standards, and *you are accepting something* you know is way below what is acceptable to you—and doing that never leads to anything good.

What was the cost for me, aside from the twelve months' worth of salary totally down the drain? The revolting feeling in my stomach every time I touched this subject with David. It ruined my day many times, at least the moment, and it altered my emotions to deal with other stuff that was important—and *I let it happen.*

Remember, "*What you focus on expands.*" If you have these negative emotions just bubbling close to the surface because of something you have the power to change immediately, then you need to stop and do something about it. You don't want more stuff like that showing up in your experience—and they will. Don't let it drag like I did in this situation and in so many others that I have lived. I learned my lesson.

Like the Tony Hsieh quote says, *"Be slow to hire and quick to fire."* Stop here.

If you have not written down your life's reason why, stop here.

I urge you to take five minutes and write it down. This will be your sustaining power over the next weeks, months, years; this is the gasoline you will need for your journey. Do not underestimate it.

Close your eyes and for a minute just picture in your mind what you want and why you want it. What does it feel like? Amplify your feelings in your mental picture to the point that you are inundated with love, gratitude, and wellbeing.

Now you are ready to write it down. Keep it close to you, and rewrite it any time you want to feel good. I do it every day in my gratitude journal before I start my day and it gives me the state that I need to be in to move through my day-to-day. No matter what comes at me, I am emotionally and mentally ready: I know what I want and I know why I want it.

"How you do anything is how you do everything."
– T. Harv Eker

Chapter 4
STEP 3-HOW WILL YOU GET IT?

WHAT DOES BEING AN EMOTIONAL
BEING REALLY MEAN IN YOUR LIFE?

By now you have a clear understanding about the role your emotions play.

Again, we are emotional beings. Our emotions are the force that shape our lives. They are what drives us to action, they are what sustains our moving forward, and when we are at the lowest point possible, emotions are what spring us back from any dark place we may be in. For some it may be hitting the lowest emotional threshold, for others it may be a lack of tolerance to "half okays" and the burning desire to have the fullest, most extraordinary experiences they can have.

You may think and pride yourself on being a very logical person, and that is good for your self-esteem. But the fact remains that what drives our behavior is conditioned reaction to pain or pleasure, not intellectual calculation. Intellectually we may believe that having that chocolate chip cookie is not very good for our health, or the Netflix series binging is a precious life waster, but we still reach for it. Why? Because it gives us immediate pleasure, even if we know it is not good.

Why do people then continue to play small and safe in their businesses? Continue to be in bad relationships? Continue in a workplace that is not remotely fulfilling? Continue to have the same low standards that dictate a life that feels like it is being wasted?

It is all because our mind literally screams every time we get out of what we know, of our comfort zone, our conditioned zone, our belief-programmed zone. It would mean sailing the unchartered waters, walking the less-travelled roads, it would mean diving into the complete unknown. For a lot of people this is terrifying. It could mean a lot more pain than the pain they are living now.

And the key word is "could mean," meaning: it has not happened, it is completely in our heads, in our imagination. Most times our worse fears are not based in past experiences but on experiences that we concoct in our minds—not real!

If we desire to have a successful business, we have to be willing to take the risks and get out of known waters. If we want deep relationships we must be willing to be vulnerable, to open our hearts. If we play safe we will remain in shallow relationships.

"Fear is the anticipation of pain." I love this definition. It allows me to take control of a situation by looking objectively at the thought that is causing me to feel fear, then proceed to just acknowledge the thought and make it ridiculous, like, "This is just a freaking delusion, it is not real, it has not happened and it never will." And move on.

THE STORY OF THE WOLF

Native American Cherokee Folklore
Rewritten by Kali Hawlk

One evening an old Cherokee chief told his grandson about a battle that goes on inside people. He said:

"My son, the battle is between two wolves inside us all. One is Evil— It is anger, envy, jealousy, sorrow, regret, greed, arrogance, self-pity, guilt, resentment, inferiority, lies, false pride, superiority, and ego.

The other is Good—It is joy, peace, love, hope, serenity, humility, kindness, benevolence, empathy, generosity, truth, compassion and faith."

The grandson thought about it for a minute and the asked his grandfather: "Which wolf wins?"

The old Cherokee simply replied, "The one you feed."

Become very conscious of your emotions. Become the observer as if detached from your body. When you have positive emotion, amplify it any way you can, and when you have a negative emotion, shift your attention somewhere else. Do not feed it, do not dwell on it, just acknowledge it. Give it a name (I feel afraid, I feel frustrated, I feel angry....) and don't go deeper into the reasons why you feel that way. Do it the same way you would with a two-year-old, divert your attention: take a five-minute walk outside your office, search "funniest pranks" or "funniest jokes" in YouTube, and forget the world for five minutes. Do anything you like at that moment; it is only five minutes, but it can make a world of difference in your emotional state. Do not let it escalate—once it gains momentum it is nearly impossible to stop the down-spiraling of negative feelings, badly taken decisions in the heat of the moment, and just plain attracting more of the same negative into your experience. Remember, *"What you focus on, expands."*

MOTIVATION VS. INSPIRATION

To a lot of people these mean the same thing. They are not.

Motivation is about psyching yourself up with external stimulants: chest-pounding, fire-walking, economic incentives, high-tempo music. You get the idea.

Inspiration, on the other hand, comes from within. Inspiration means "to-be-in-spirit." This is when you are aligned with your spirit, when you feel like you are *"tuned-in, tapped-in, and turned-on to your higher self,"* as Abraham Hicks tells us. It is when whatever you are thinking or doing feels so good and time disappears. It is what is known as the state of *Flow* as stated by positive psychologist Mihály Csíkszentmihályi.

This alone is one of the main reasons why 96 percent of new businesses disappeared by year ten.

Motivation is when you feel you should be doing something, when you feel that you are "supposed" to be doing something. It often leads to just being "busy." It gives you the illusion that you are doing a lot, but the truth is that it is often focused on really irrelevant things that won't cause the big impact you desire. These things you do when you try to motivate yourself with a titan's willpower often leave you tired and overwhelmed. Today you crossed ten things off your to-do list, tomorrow it will be fifteen … is a day-to-day grinding.

You are an entrepreneur. The idea of hard work does not make you shrink. You believe smart work and determination will pay off eventually—it is what we entrepreneurs are made of. So why does it feel so freaking hard!?!

It has to do with *Inspiration*. When you feel inspired you are called to action. When you, first and foremost, come to really realize who you are in your full potential, versus the limited being you sometimes may believe you are. You will feel ready to undertake anything you want, you will feel excited, and most important, you will feel an impulse to act, which then can turn into a nagging feeling that will propel you to action. You will be pulled and you will soar in your flow!

You know you are inspired when…

- Life feels effortless; it feels like it happens with a natural ease.
- You have to hold yourself back from acting right now.
- Your passion grows, evolves steadily, it does not get consumed.
- You are constantly thinking about whatever is holding your attention. It does not feel like research or study. Even in your "free time" you can't stop thinking about it.
- You feel it in your bones. You have such clarity that it is undeniable to you.
- You don't see problems, just mere things that need to be done, period. With ease.
- You feel not only optimistic, but also a sense of certain expectation.

"HOW DO I GET INSPIRED?"

You cannot. Inspiration is not something you get from outside (that is motivation, remember?) Inspiration comes from within. It is about aligning your conscious self with your higher-self, inner-self, spirit.

And alignment is about a constant process. It is not something you obtain once and are done. When you feel frustrated and stuck in your business, it is time to realign. When you feel stressed (which is just "fear" in businessman terms) it is time to realign. When you just feel like giving up, it is time to realign.

And to realign is rather very easy. You just need to go inside, explore inward. Pause and think about what you really want. What is it that lights you up? What do you love to do? Think of moments when you have felt happy, joyful, content … close your eyes and bask in the feeling of it all, embrace it, fuel it with gratitude and appreciation.

Smile with your eyes closed. Feel the warmth that spreads from your chest all over your body. Breathe deeply and smile again.

Does it feel good? It sure does. If you don't, you are not yet there. Just keep going a bit longer.

Once you are there, then you are *In-Spirit*. You are inspired. You now have the state to have clarity, to eagerly take action. This is when it stops feeling so hard to make it work!

It is a practice, it is what I like to call "working out the muscle of happiness." It takes the focus and the time to do it, until you make it into a habit.

Having a clear understanding of the differences between Motivation and Inspiration, my take is the following: I like to leverage the use of both.

I have spent over $100,000 in courses, coaching, making affirmation moves, walking on fire, Cherokee sweat lodges, singing, dancing, high elevation challenges, putting a fire torch out with my mouth, bending iron bars with my neck, intense camps … you name it, I have done it!

These are all part of external stimulants; these are motivational activities. They have worked wonders in my life; I go to them and I feel re-charged. If you want real changes in the fastest way, the best way of doing it is with someone who has been there and done that. Someone to know the shorts cuts, the insights, to hold the space for you to transform with love and compassion while at the same time holding you 100% accountable for your decisions and actions.

The best of both worlds is what I do, constantly.

I go to the events and one-on-one coaching programs to have that powerful motivation, and I practice my in-spirit alignment and daily habits every single day. This is my paving the way to start the day.

Mastering this practice, little by little, will help you transform yourself and obtain the results you work so hard for.

PAVING THE WAY – THREE GOLDEN RULES

"How can I elevate my state and my vibrations when I don't feel good at all? I have to drag myself out of bed and the thought of another day at my own business, dealing with problems and more problems, just sucks the life out of me. Every day seems the same. It is a constant struggle to juggle everything and keep it going."

It is all about *momentum*, moving forward, little by little.

So, since it is moving forward on purpose, would you set reverse shift on purpose? Of course not! Right?

We have talked about how to raise our physical and emotional state. How about if we discuss how to, at the very least and as a point of starting our journey, not shift to reverse when we want to move forward.

So, let me tell you about my Three Golden Rules.

GOLDEN RULE 1 – Don't Complain

Every time you complain about anything in your life—whether it is your pain-in-the-butt client or something as simple as running out of sugar for your coffee—catch yourself and stop! I am serious, we tend to complain out of habit. Many times it is just conditioned reactions that we've had over many years.

When you complain, it immediately brings down your energy levels and your serotonin (the feel good hormone) levels. When you put those glasses on and you notice so many things "wrong," it gains momentum and one little thing turns into many little things for you to complain about. Then it will turn into a full avalanche of things to complain about. Sound familiar?

Challenge #1 – The Seven Day Challenge

Get a rubber band and place it on your left wrist (or your right if you are a leftie). Every time you complain, stretch the rubber band away from your wrist and let go.

Yeap! You will be flogging yourself. This is no S&M class to feel good, but just like Pavlov with his dog experiments, you are conditioning yourself to change a behavior. This is done either with a reward or a punishment.

So, let's just say that I would like to tweak it and instead of punishment I would like to call it physical awareness of a non-physical behavior (complaining, that is) so that every time you complain and hurt yourself you realize how many times a day you are actually complaining. I would ask you to make a journal and contemplate it, but that is just plain passive and boring to me—nothing really is at stake.

The first day you will have an irritated wrist, that I can guarantee you. When I first did this exercise, I did so enthusiastically, I ended up with many tiny red spots at the end of the day, bits of blood coming out … I was not going to die of it, but it proved a point, a very important point.

Here comes the good news: after day three, you will barely use the rubber band.

And this is because at a very subconscious level your mind's main job is to preserve your physical integrity. You will notice that you may have the thought to complain, but seconds before you say something you will remember pain of the rubber band and you will stop your mouth from opening and uttering any words.

When the days pass and you keep your intention of not complaining, something short of miraculous starts to happen: you stop having thoughts of complaints.

Or just when you are about to have them, you stop yourself and think twice. You become the observer of your behavior, and the one making the decisions about it. When this happens, you are making a *huge* change in your vibration, in your feeling-good state, and in our consciousness. I will say again, you become the observer.

It does not take only seven days to stop complaining for the rest of your life. It takes practice and deliberate focus on your part, but you actually just began to change your neuropaths—that is, the way you usually think and thus behave, the way you usually feel, your set point.

Seven days is a test run if you will. In seven days you can have a taste of what it feels like not to complain in a mindless way—and I can tell you, it feels great!

Besides, something absolutely fantastic also happens: you become more likable! Yes, there is a powerful saying that I love and helps me every time I feel I want to complain:

"There are two types of people: those who affect people in a positive way or those who infect people. Which type are you?"

You can make the choice, right now. Get a rubber band.

GOLDEN RULE 2 – Do Not Criticize

When you criticize others it also takes your state of being down. When you are judging someone you are really bringing more of what you are criticizing to your experience. There are some aspects about criticizing that I would like to bring to your attention.

First: there is the psychological effect called the Chameleon Effect, which states that people behave unconsciously the way that others expect them to behave. This is quite amazing. Have you ever noticed how you are funny with a particular person? And how you tend to be more prompt to anger with another person? With some people you feel smart and witty and with others you feel slow witted, even dumb? Yet you are the same person with the attributes that you know you have. Why do you behave differently, then?

It has to do with what *they* expect of you. There is an energy exchange all the time, whether you know it or not, whether you understand it or not, whether you accept it or not, it is how it is, scientifically proven by our modern Quantum Physics.

So, when you criticize, you are reinforcing the behavior that they show with you that you are criticizing (they are not like that with everyone, but with you they are!). You are giving attention to the aspects that you don't like, that are falling short of your expectations. When you put your attention and intensive focus on this, it will gain momentum and expand!

"What you focus on expands!" It is a Law.

It is not only Quantum Physics by the book, but it is a common thing you see happening every day. This is by far one of my favorite new acquired beliefs—"new" meaning for about the past twelve years—that I keep repeating to myself. And remember, a belief is nothing more than a thought you repeat often until it becomes your truth.

On the other hand, has anyone you know improved their behavior due to your criticizing them relentlessly? And if they did, were they able to sustain that new "improved" behavior? Very unlikely, I would think.

Second: what you say and observe about others says a lot more about you than about them.

> *"Beauty (or ugliness) is in the eye of the beholder."*
> **– Unknown**

Something to think about, no?

If I criticize an employee at my office, what does that say about me? What am I lacking as a leader? Could it be clearer communication? Could it be that I need to establish clear job expectations and boundaries? Could it be that I need to work on my appreciation for the good things that this person brings to the table?

And, if there is nothing, absolutely nothing that you see that is good in this person, or in any given situation, then take action about it. *"We get in life what we tolerate."* Do what is in your hands to fix the problem from the root. But stop criticizing and judging.

Become part of the solution, or simply shut up.

It is like "Trying to kill someone with poison but drinking it yourself." Would it work?

Third: Criticizing puts you in a frequency of lack of compassion and lack of appreciation.

What do you actually gain by this? You will never change who or what you are judging this way. You will not feel better about it; it will not improve how you feel. And like complaining, criticizing is also a mindless bad habit, acquired after many years of doing it. For many people it becomes a conversation opener. This happens to me at my children's school more often than not: "Hi Lina, did you see how badly the teacher organized this activity?" "Lunch is really bad, don't you think?" "Hey, good morning! I have been waiting thirty minutes to park! The school should do something about it!" or "Hey, how are you? What did you think of the teacher's speech? Gee … she could learn a bit more about how to speak to the parents." Really???

Can you change your bad habit of criticizing? Absolutely!

Challenge #2 – The Seven Day Challenge
Yes, Again

Buy another rubber band, a different color, and do the same exercise for seven days. This time the goal is not to criticize or judge others.

GOLDEN RULE 3 – Do Not Blame Others or Circumstances

So this one is the one that trips us up the most, since we tend to believe that the people and circumstances that surround us determine our reality and the events that happen in our lives.

This is when you say, "I am not happy because …" (fill in the blank: my husband, my wife, my children, my boss, my friend, my pet, my government) is always … (fill in the blank: controlling me, blaming it on me, disrespecting me, stabbing me in the back, destroying and peeing on my furniture, increasing the freaking taxes….)

Yet, the truth is that you create your life. *Only YOU.*

"We are the direct result of 10 percent of our circumstances and 90% how we react to it."

Situations will always come up, it is part of life. It is not only unavoidable but at some point we come to realize that, thanks to those situations, we actually got something good out of it and we became more in the process. You can choose to go a lifetime blaming others for what happened, or you can really take a look and change the meaning that you gave the story, what it meant for you then, and what it means for you now. Let go of what does not serve you anymore and embrace the lesson as a treasure.

STORY OF TWO SOLDIERS

One soldier went to the War of Afghanistan. He was a sniper and his best buddy was his spotter. One day on a mission, they were ambushed without warning. The experience was terrifying and, just when they were about to be pulled out, his friend got a direct hit to his head. The soldier's best friend's brains spilled all over him.

The other soldier went also to a war, the Iraq War. He was a Navy Seal. One day on a mission in enemy territory, his teammate and best buddy was walking ahead of him. He stepped on a mine and blew himself to pieces right in front of the soldier.

Eventually, each soldier went back home.

The first soldier got reclusive and never got close to anyone again in his life. He swore to himself that he was not going to get hurt again. He was lonely and bitter. His life was empty and meaningless.

The second soldier decided that life was too short and that he wanted to cherish each person he had in his life to the fullest; he wanted each minute to count. He had a life filled with love and appreciation for all the people in his life. He was happy and life was meaningful to him.

Both had the same experience but the decision that each made to give meaning to the event was radically different and it led to a radically different life.

Can you see how it is up to you to make a decision about how you want to see what happens around you? Life is not happening to you, life is happening for you. Whatever the circumstances in your life have been or are, if you are going to choose a story through which to see it, choose one that empowers you, that make you bigger, that makes you stronger! You can choose—no one but you can make you choose your thoughts, that is where your power resides.

At this point in the book you have learned the importance of having a crystal-clear vision of where you want to go (Step1). You also walked through the process of understanding the pivotal importance of your *reason why* and writing it down for your future inspiration tool when you need to remember and fuel yourself again (Step 2). Then we proceeded to Step 3, where we explored the *how to get it,* where it was made clear that as an emotional being it is your mental and emotional state that determine the actions you choose. I will repeat the words of my mentor, Tony Robbins: *"Success is 80 percent psychology and 20 percent strategy and mechanics."* We focused on the 80 percent psychology part of it in Step 3.

If you are here, well done!! You are way ahead of the 95 percent of the people who never really question their lives and just keep rolling mindlessly. They witness how the same patterns of the things they don't like keep showing up in their lives and wonder why these experiences keep happening. You are now way past this, well done!

You now know that you deliberately decide your destination. You decide how to live your present, you decide if you want to become the master of your thoughts and emotions, and then you will without a doubt grow your business. You will feel excited and will stay motivated.

One step at a time, consistently, until you reached your mastery level. You become it by living it. It is your decision.

Chapter 5

STEP 4 - UNDERSTANDING WHAT PREVENTS YOU WHAT IS SLOWING YOU DOWN?

A belief is nothing more than words you've told yourself so often it became your truth.

A belief is nothing more than words you've been told so often by others that at some point you accepted it as your truth.

The big problem: these so-called "truths" by you are now seated in the deepest part of your subconscious, they are your programs, they are the conditioned part in you.

You may not even be completely aware of them; I mean to say, you may not even be able to put them into words if I asked you what your most predominant beliefs are about this or that. But when you have an automatic response, a reaction (and this is 95 percent of your time—you are just "running an established subconscious program") these come from that deep-seated belief system you have.

There are information bibles out there that can explain to you how a belief is formed and what it means in your life. My two favorite mentors, authors with scientific backgrounds, are Joe Dispenza and Bruce Lipton. I invite you to check what they have to say regarding your beliefs, and how your conscious and subconscious mind works. You will be astounded and it will also help you recognize and explain your current patterns of behavior like it did for me.

I am going to make it real simple though: everything, and I mean *everything*, every thought or word you say to yourself that makes you feel bad, that makes you feel small, that makes you feel disempowered, *is not true.*

It is not—no matter how "reality" shows you over and over again evidence to the contrary, believe me—it is not true. If it does not serve you, it is not true.

It is not a true belief, it is a delusion on your part.

Yes, you read that right, a delusion, like the ones you are now thinking that only lunatics or crazy people in mad houses have.

Why would you think that anything that does not serve you is the truth???

Say, if you think you are not confident enough, not smart enough, not good enough, not persuasive enough, not worthy enough … well, understand that life will mirror these to you in your experiences and it will make you think it is real, but it is totally not.

Why is it not real? Simple: your present does not equate your future. Your present does not equate your future. Your present does not equate your future. This is not a typo—I meant to repeat it three times. If you only internalize this into your core beliefs you are way, way ahead of the game and ready to take the next steps.

The good news: you can change it all. You can change your program—yeap, the software you are running you can change any time. Will it be immediate? No, it will not. Because the only way to change a deeply-rooted false delusion or false belief is by repetition.

And repetition takes time!

Repetition of your new beliefs that empower you and make you feel good and repetition of new habits that help you transform your emotional, spiritual, and physical body. See, it is both a mental exercise to change your new beliefs (remember, the muscle of happiness) and a physical exercise when you decide to acquire new empowering habits that support your new beliefs.

This takes time, at least sixty-six days, as new scientific studies are showing. But what are sixty-six days to a better, bigger, and more fulfilled you? You can close the gap between where you are and where you want to be, but the very first thing you will need to work on are your beliefs—your disempowering beliefs, that is.

Your conscious self is where all your creativity lies, is where your power is, *but* your subconscious self is where your habitual self resides, where your old programs are running. Just saying with clarity what you want and why you want it is a fantastic place to start, it is your Life GPS being turned on, but at some point you will need to take action.

And taking action, when you are saying to yourself: *ready, set and go!* Will you go? Will you spring with all your might and passion forward? Sometimes not, or maybe even most of the time in certain areas of your life.

We only spend 5 percent of our time in our creative and powerful consciousness. This is when you are awake and you are very mindful of what is going on around you and are directing your thoughts. You are the observer, you are the programmer when you are in this state.

The only way you can achieve transformation is when you stop your automatic reactions in the other 95 percent of your awake time (the old talk, delusions) and begin being present and deliberately take new actions based on new thoughts and emotions. Through repetition of words and habits you rewrite your new program. It is the only way and it *requires the Zen Warrior in you: to conquer your own self.*

Another critical difference between the conscious mind and the subconscious mind is the fact that they learn in different ways. The conscious mind, being creative, learns in the moment, reading a book, attending a seminar, watching a video, experiencing something. Now, subconscious mind being the habitual self, by definition it will not change easily. The only way that it will change is by repetition. And here we are again. Repetition of empowering thoughts to create a new you and repetition of new habits to support these new thoughts.

The biggest challenge is that you may think that when you become aware of something new you will immediately adopt it, just by being aware of it in your conscious mind. Scientifics tell us it does not work that way at all (Bruce Lipton has a fantastic book on this if you want to expand your knowledge: *The Biology of Belief*). Repetition is needed to break an old habit and replace it with one that is new and helps you take those next steps to bring it to the new level you so desire.

Remember: "Repetition is the mother of all skills."

It is not an impossible task—you just need to do it.

FAKE IT UNTIL YOU MAKE IT!

Small tip worth a million dollars: when in doubt, fake it.

Like you've heard, *"Fake it until you make it."* I know that it may sound icky, but I will tell you something: your brain does not know the difference between what is real (what you can see and feel on the outside with your senses) and what is not yet real.

In your mental world all thoughts trigger a response and will release hormones depending on the thoughts you are having, whether they serve you or not. If you are having happy and positive thoughts then your brain releases oxytocin (the love hormone), dopamine (the reward hormone), endorphins (the calm hormone) and serotonin (the willpower hormone) and you will feel inspired, at peace, aligned, and excited.

In the complete opposite direction, when you think negative thoughts (which most of the time are fears of events that have not even happened in your life) your body will be flooded with the hormones of stress and fear: cortisol and adrenaline.

Just know: you are the master, you are the pilot, you need to become very aware of your daily thoughts, they determine your life. If your thoughts determine the hormones you are releasing into your body and these hormones determine how you feel, then how you feel determines your actions and your actions determine your results, then it may really be worth your while to get into the habit of observing your most recurrent thoughts.

BELIEFS > THOUGHTS > FEELINGS > ACTION = LIFE RESULTS

When you practice faking it until you make it (especially in terms of actions), you are already paving the way at a deep level of the subconscious for how to change a belief (remember: a belief is nothing more than what you have repeated so many times it became your truth) and then a change in automatic behavior will follow.

I remember when I was just beginning my executive career. I was the director of Customer Service and Operations at a very young and still inexperienced age, twenty-seven. I was asked many times to go to board meetings and present the company's strategies and results in my area. I did not know this saying then, but still I decided in my mind that I was going to play a role the minute I walked into those board meetings with all the big shots of the company. I was going to be "an actress portraying a very confident, knowledgeable, brilliant, and witty executive" and I was going to tell "the real Lina" to just go to a happy place, somewhere else far from the board, for the next two hours. I did it, and it worked wonders every single time. And then, something wonderful happened: I became that person. I don't even know at what point exactly, but I was not freaking out every time I had to speak in public to present anything. And now I enjoy it tremendously.

Think about it: if I tell you right now to act like a medieval king while you are addressing your subjects, wouldn't you assume the stance, the sureness, the sort of condescending powerful look one imagines a king would have? Even the words you chose would be different. It is exactly the same when you play it in your real life, portraying a confident person, a fearless person, a successful person, a smart person (the easiest! Just listen and ask questions), anything. You just need to do it until you naturally become it.

Again, remember: *"Repetition is the mother of all skills."*

The meaning we give everything, every single thing we label "good or bad," depends on the lenses we have on to view life. These are our beliefs, and a belief is just a thought or an idea we keep repeating ourselves, or that we have heard many times, until it becomes our truth. These beliefs were acquired through our experiences, mostly during our childhood (which is the time when we have no filter and our parents and teachers teach us that grown-up know better—sometimes I doubt this very much).

We could learn a lot from a five year old: how all they do is seek the moment of joy in the present, have fun, nature is a wonder to them, they easily make friends, crying is quickly forgotten, they trust, they are kind to animals, they easily love … so many things that grown-ups have forgotten; it is there, but for many it is buried under layers upon layers of very disempowering and weakening beliefs that lead to small lives one settles for and not the amazing life one can deliberately choose.

REALLY?!?

Some time ago I read something that shocked me at the moment and made me stop and really take a look. The phrase read something like, "Most of your beliefs, your truths, what rules your life are your parents' opinions." Opinions?!?! What!?

If you think about it, what you heard over and over when you were a child was everybody's opinions on everything, and that stays with you: the ones you hear the most and the ones you especially see the most behavior about.

It is through those lenses that you will see your life. I was just a bit sick with the thought … my life's truths were somebody else's opinions? Makes you think, no? Then it makes you really want to revisit these beliefs you have, evaluate them, and decide which have empowered you and which have definitely not.

ANOTHER TAKE: PAIN VS. SUFFERING

"Pain is unavoidable, suffering is optional."

Imagine a woman giving birth to her firstborn, eight hours of long and intensive labor. Did she suffer? No. Why? Because of the meaning she gave to the event: the person she would give her life for was being born that day. For sure there were tears, for sure there was almost unbearable physical pain … but suffering? None at all. Would she do it again? Yes.

She experienced emotional and physical pain giving birth, but she can recall this experience as one of total love and unending care for her newborn. That is the meaning she gave to the pain, therefore there is no suffering involved—none, whatsoever. She will not dwell in the pain.

It did happen, but it has no negative emotional attachments to it. On the contrary, the emotional attachments are those of immense love and gratitude.

This is the best example I once heard from my sister-in-law Dana Benarroch—well known corporate transformational coach and speaker in my country—to describe the difference between pain and suffering.

Life will always bring us events and circumstances that are viewed as painful: losing a job, a divorce, the death of a loved one, personal sickness, losing all financial means, living in a country with no freedom of opportunities, and so many other instances.

These events are part of our regular existence, are part of life. *It is the meaning we give these events, the stories we attach to these events, that shape our lives, our decisions, and how we view the world around us.*

The events and circumstances did happen; I am not saying that we should try to forget them or avoid them. On the contrary, if you acknowledge that the event happened and you embrace it and look at it as an observer and derive from it a higher meaning to you and those around you, this event can and will make you a better version or yourself.

"What we focus on expands and what we resist, persists."

When I lost our home and investment properties in the real state crisis of 2008, I felt totally defeated. I felt guilty, I blamed myself and the institutions. I was sorely resentful of the Universe. *"I worked so hard and I am a good person. How did this happen to me? I have always done everything by the book. Why?"*

Then I realized, okay, this is what I have created, this is my reality. Yes there are millions who were affected, but there were also millions of people who were not. What am I creating in my life, where is my attention going to? What are my most predominant thoughts and feelings? And second and most important: what did I learn from this? I promised myself that I would get into real estate again. When I mentioned this to some of my friends, they taught I was crazy!

One year later we were buying our home again and later we got into property investment again. I learned the lessons, I was doing better this time around, and the guilt and anger I felt when contemplating that huge loss was gone and instead replaced by another big realization: the worst that I thought could happen, happened! And it was not the end of the world. Life went on, the moment passed, and I became a better and bigger person in the process.

Also, one thing I clearly noticed is that my "perception of the problem level" had dramatically decreased. What used to feel like a level ten problem, now was a level four problem, for example, if you were to use a one to ten scale for how big or little any problem is.

Yes, I still have level four problems. Still, it is my unwavering commitment to my personal growth that makes me tackle this on a daily basis, without guilt, with love toward myself and with the total understanding and acceptance that all is good as it is, and that all that happens is part of my journey. A beautiful journey to happiness and joy in the *now*, without making it conditional to external situations.

So instead of measuring how big the problem is, I now measure how big I am in relation to the problem. That is my journey.

WRITE YOUR NEW STORY

What is your story? Is there anything in your story that falls way below what you want?

Think about which area of your life you want to experience the biggest breakthrough in. Since you are reading this book, the odds are that it's about regaining excitement in your life and business, making more money in your business, living a happier and more joyful life with the ones you love. So, stop and think, why haven't these things happened yet? Why do you think this has been so? What are the reasons you think are behind it? Most likely you will write a series of events. That's good, that is part of it, but what are the real reasons, emotionally speaking, you think these events have not materialized yet? Be honest, don't make excuses of justifications, or go into denial or blame others.

What stands in the way of your dreams?

Could it be possible that in writing your story you can realize the negative impact that your story may have on you? Take a moment to assess its impact by answering some of these questions:

- *Has your story diminished or possibly destroyed your confidence and lowered your self-esteem?*
- *Has it prevented you from creating more wealth with your ideas?*
- *Has it made you angry and vengeful?*
- *Has it kept you living in fear, doubt, confusion? Or maybe going to therapy or craving outside stimulants?*
- *Has it cost you your health, your peace of mind, your joy, your business, or a relationship?*
- *Has it stopped you from really developing the most important relationship you will ever have in your life: the one with yourself?*
- *Has it prevented you from being the parent you want to be? The son you want to be? The husband you want to be?*
- *Has it blinded you to be the man or woman you want to be?*

Maybe you have answered yes to one or more of these questions. If this is so, then write what has it cost you in your life? Remember, everything that has happened to you is old news! It does not determine your future at all.

You can change that by changing the way you look at what has happened to you and the meaning that you gave it. The lessons, the new you, has to be bigger and better after going through so many experiences, but only you determine the lesson learned. Do not make the lesson one that diminishes you; on the contrary, all is good, no matter how bad you experienced it. You can now look back and learn from it.

DESPAIR = SUFFERING–MEANING

Viktor E. Frankl, the renowned psychologist who wrote *Man's Search for Meaning*, experienced the unbearable at a concentration camp during World War II, his mother, father, brother, and pregnant wife were killed in the camps and he spent years in horrific circumstances. He made a deliberate decision about how to respond to his circumstances then. After all he went through there he decided to change the meaning he gave his experience. He survived and he is a true testament to the meaning of resilience and of giving meaning to pain suffered.

He tells us in very detailed form of his experience, and he comes to show that the only way one gets into despair is when the pain endured has no meaning to the person going through the tragic event.

When you derive meaning from your pain, *the suffering stops and it transforms into a human victory of survival and expansion of self.* You become your own hero, you have your own victory—sure, there are scars, but you can proudly present them and teach others from your place of light and love to yourself.

You become more in the process and you come to realize that what is most important in life is within you already. There is nothing that can stop you if you become aware of your immense power of resilience, of creation, of love, of appreciation, of compassion, of believing in yourself first and foremost.

> *"Between stimulus and response there is a space. In that space is our power to choose our response. In our response lies our growth and our freedom."*
> – **Viktor Frankl**

Serenity Prayer

"God, grant me the SERENITY to accept the things
I cannot change, COURAGE to change the things
I can, and the WISDOM to know the difference."
– **Reinhold Niebuhr**

YOUR MIND'S PRIMARY ROLE
IS TO PROTECT YOUR INTEGRITY

Your mind does not know whether where you are is the best place in the world or the lowest, most depressing one. Its only purpose is to keep you in the "known and safe zone" and anything outside of this will make it send you bone chilling shrieks and terrifying images of all the things that could go wrong if you step out.

Your mind knows you better than anyone, knows your darkest secrets, and believe me, it will play very dirty to stop you in your tracks.

How many times have you dreaded doing something and, when you muster the courage to do it (or when life pushes you to do it!), you end up thinking, "That was not so bad and hard after all." Countless times, I am sure.

When we lost our properties between 2008 and 2010, it took us almost three years to make the decision to just let go of them and initiate what is called a short-sale. The properties values were completely upside down and for two of them we had special assessments imposed thanks to the damages of Hurricane Wilma. Just in the assessments, we lost about $100,000 because we did not make the decision to short sale quick enough.

Why? Because we were really afraid of having both of our credit scores destroyed and we did not want to have that in our record. They said it would take at least five years to recover. At the end, after bleeding dollars for three years, we made the decision to short sale, and guess what? Less than eighteen months later I was receiving pre-approval letters for new credit cards! It was not nearly as painful and bad as we thought it would be. Yeap, lesson: I should have done it sooner. Expensive lesson learned.

This chapter has shown you how the decisions you make in your day-to-day are closely linked to avoidance of pain or seeking of pleasure in your life. This is of utmost importance because by changing your pain/pleasure associations in your mind, you can change your actions and therefore the outcomes in your life: your destiny.

What stops you from moving forward? Allow me to push you a bit again here.

In the previous section there were a few questions to help you identify where you are in regards to your story; they were not there as rhetorical questions to help illustrate a point. My intention with those questions was that you take five minutes to answer them as quickly as you can (the more thinking you put into the equation, the more you are framing your answers—just write what comes out spontaneously). Time it. Once you are done, analyze what you wrote and really evaluate how much of that has helped you in your life or how much of that story has slowed you down.

Change your thoughts, change your life. Create your new story. Write what you learned, how it made you stronger, or how that story made you derive more clarity in your life. Remember, there is no better time in your life to know what you want than when you have experienced a negative situation. Clarity is a very powerful and inspiring state of mind and being.

Chapter 6

STEP 5 – SUCCESS
HOW WILL YOU KNOW
YOU HAVE SUCCEEDED?

WHAT DOES SUCCESS MEAN TO YOU?

To *me* it means:

1. Achieving my personal, professional and spiritual goals in my regular day-to-day, while living a life with a sense of purpose and fulfillment.

The first time we decided to embark in Delivering Happiness at ALO as our philosophy platform for our company culture, both David and I felt afraid of "*what if some of them decide to leave?*" All of our employees, without exception, were wonderful human beings, highly skilled and with years of experience with our company and our products.

To launch this new company philosophy, we decided to do our first company retreat, 100 percent of the employees on a three-day retreat with the main topic Happiness.

Of course all the conferences, workshops, and activities revolved around, "Are you happy? Do you know what makes you happy? Do you know what you want? Do you know your passions?" And so on.

So, imagine us thinking, *"What if we facilitate the space for them to go really deep within and some of them leave? I don't want to start hiring and training!"*

These thoughts and feelings quickly passed and we realized that yeah, this was a possibility, and if it happened, no matter how big "the loss" was, the gaining was much, much bigger for everyone, including us. If anyone decided that ALO was not his/her place, then good for them and their new path, and good for the company—you really want people with their heart and soul in your business, helping you.

No one left then, and in all the *Familia ALO* retreats we have done over the past eight years, only one person resigned because she realized after the event that this was not what she wanted to be doing in her life and that she wanted to pursue other passions. She was deeply grateful to us for helping her realize what she really wanted in her life.

Every time I lead one of these events with David, I feel immense appreciation, love, and gratitude for everyone. I give 100 percent of my heart during those three days in the conferences and workshops I organize and actively participate in, and I only want my employees to have a happier life. I want them to remember who they really are and I guide them through the steps that have served me and countless others in how they can create their own magnificent lives.

I often see people transforming right there, having fantastic insights and "aha moments," and I know right there that that aspect of their lives will never be the same.

I get in return a sense of fulfillment and life purpose beyond what words can express.

And, what type of impact do you think this type of employee transformation (and yours) would have in your business? On your bottom line?

Remember: *"Achievement without fulfillment is the ultimate failure."*

You totally get the concept; you now know that the end of the road is about expanding who you are. It is about the person you need to become in order to reach your business goals, contribute to others, and embrace the day as it comes, all ups and downs are part of the picture.

The ups are great—they show you how well you are creating your reality, how well you are being the master of your thoughts and managing your powerful and creating magnetic feelings. The downs are great too! They show your point of creation of the now so that you can make corrections before it continues to build up. What an amazing and accurate navigation system (our emotions) we all have!

Business growth, financial abundance has reached our door, but it has been much sweeter being accompanied by personal fulfillment. Achieve your financial goals, it is all within your reach. It is your birthright to come to this life to experience and enjoy it to the fullest, and that is not in philosophical terms—no! It means to enjoy all abundance and crazy fun that money can provide: all the new experiences, the savoring of this delicious life, are your birthright. Own it, it is yours.

And then ... give back, love back, teach, inspire, guide, care, make the world a better place. You can start with your immediate circle of influence: yourself and your employees.

Do it not just because productivity will be increased if they are happier, or because they will go the extra mile or because there will be a lower personnel turnover, among many other corporate benefits. Do it because you are helping individuals have a better quality of life, to be happy whether they remain in your company or they eventually move on.

It is the only way to feel fulfilled—when you put yourself at the service of others. You don't need to become Mother Theresa, but in anything you do, big or small, having their best interests in your heart will make you feel really good, and that doesn't have a price.

2. Living my life without regrets

Imagine yourself when you are eighty years old, nearing the end of your life. You are sitting in your rocking chair, reflecting on how you lived your life. Now, look back on your life as if you had not achieved the goals you are after at this moment in your life. How has this affected the course of your life? What are your regrets? What do you wish you had made more time for? What do you wish you had tried? Is there sadness and regret? Are you wondering, "what if...."?

When I have put myself in this scenario and picture myself at eighty pondering about my life, the recurring fear has always been that of unfulfilled potential. There is nothing that I fear more than regretting not doing something because I was afraid, even if I knew I had everything that it takes to do it. This thought of unfulfilled potential has inspired me to take the first step on many occasions.

Some years ago it used to be fear of failure, but over the years I have learned to be grateful for my failures. They have taught me valuable life lessons. They have formed my character and they have given me resilience. And most especially, they have shown me in clear precise ways those things that I am not willing to tolerate anymore. They helped me raise my standards.

Now in my life I am getting to a point where I truly believe *that all is well as it is.* That I can move forward while giving a "lower level of importance" to many things, from a more serene place, because I feel the certainty that things are already accomplished without constant push from my part. I trust that I am not alone, and I trust in the power of my thoughts.

What moves me more than anything now is the feeling of joy, purpose, and fulfillment in what I choose to do every day. And when I am not quite there, I go back to my exercises to get there. It is the way of the Zen Business Warrior: conquering one's self.

So I always move forward. I take the first step and the Universe shows me ways—people, circumstances, things—and then I take massive action to make things happen and make sure to keep my personal and business skills sharp.

I live a life with no regrets; that is one measure of success to me.

Do you?

3. Living my life in equilibrium

This is probably the biggest aspect in my life I consciously focus my attention to: to live a balanced life. And it is one that I am profoundly proud to have achieved and one that I am immensely grateful for every day.

Getting into my forties has probably had a lot to do with it. I have lived moments of imbalance, putting too much attention over long periods of time on aspects that seemed to be very important (success measured by others or society's standards, what others thought of me or what others expected of me, for example), but were actually not. At the time, my sense of urgency got mixed up a lot with my sense of importance.

This happens when you don't take a deep look at all the aspects of what make up your life and determine where you are and where you really need and want to be in each important aspect of your life.

I love my life! I love where I am and I love the expectation of what is yet to come.

I have consciously worked on having a life in equilibrium and I now live the manifestation of it all. I am grateful and appreciative beyond what words can express.

EQUILIBRIUM

Everything in the Universe seeks equilibrium, everything seeks balance.

There is equilibrium in giving and receiving. Our human body is a perfect machine that seeks equilibrium. There is balance in nature, in the plants, the animals, the climate. It all works in perfect balance and harmony. We are part of the Universe. We also need to be in balance to experience life to the fullest, to feel fully alive and wholesome mentally, physically, emotionally, and spiritually.

Remember, where attention goes, energy flows.

Balance is something that needs to be done consciously and permanently to be able to sustain a well-lived life.

What is business success to you if you lose your health in the process? Or if you lose your spouse and children? What if you work so hard that you neglect your body? You may not be sick, but maybe by seven p.m. you are half dead? What about fun? Amazing sex? Friends? Hobbies? Are you always saying, "Later, I don't have time now? Or I don't have the energy …"

Well, this is your wakeup call: Life is what happens while you are planning it.

Yes, in business there come times when we need the energy of the Warrior, the do-whatever-it-takes-attitude, the burning of the bridges spirit that leaves nothing on the table. Yes, there are times that require that, when it is no longer a *should do* but a *must do, must have, must become.*

The problem: it is not a 100-meter sprint; it is a marathon.

The prize: your happiness, your peace of mind, and your fulfillment.

The question: what is *really* important to you? Your business is *only* the means to an end. What is your end? Are you afraid that if you *relax and ease* a bit you will lose your business? You may lose something far more important than your business, than money, if you are not in equilibrium.

THE WHEEL OF LIFE

The Wheel of Life is a way to take a good, hard look at each facet of your life and rate its relative quality level, so you can uncover which areas need more attention than others. Think of each area like a spoke of a wheel: when one of the spokes is shorter than the others, it can throw the whole thing off balance.

By getting a clear visual of every aspect of your life, you can identify where you are doing amazingly well and where there is room for improvement—to discover where the gaps are between where you are today and where you want to be.

No matter how accomplished or happy we are, we all have areas of our lives that could use some improvement—and in most cases, different amounts of improvement. Think about your health, for instance. Are you in a peak state of health, feeling energetic and full of vitality? If so, congratulations! But now move on to another area: personal finance. Are you on the right track to achieve financial freedom? What about your personal relationships? Do you feel loved and supported? Do you love and support your family, your loved ones? Do you have activities that infuse fun into your life?

Too many people are caught up with making a living instead of taking the time to design their lives and making sure they keep them on track.

To be able to consciously design your life, you need to have a map. First to mark where you are, and second, to see where you want to go.

The Wheel is a great and easy exercise for you to do this. It is misleadingly simple, yet very powerful. It will give you a visual that you can keep and in a few months you can do it again and compare, and keep doing it until you reach your goal.

Everything you express by writing is a decree to the Universe and is a commitment to yourself. Make your word Law. *You can always choose to do or not to do.* Don't say, "I will try." Most of the time this leads to giving yourself an excuse (from the beginning) that you are just "trying your best".

T. Harv Eker tells us in his book *Secrets of the Millionaire Mind* that saying "I will try" and finding an excuse (or justification in your mind) would just create the *Habit of Failure.* This is when you get so used to not doing what you say you will that it just does not bother you so much anymore. You have the habit of failure activated in your subconscious and you have learned to tolerate it and accept it. This is what being mediocre means: just trying your best.

You can choose not to do it. It is a choice—you just need to accept the cost of not attaining what you desire, accept it 100 percent, and live a happy life.

For example, if you are 150 pounds overweight and you come to decide that you will not lose the weight, that's fine—as long as you decide to be happy and you accept, for instance, that you may not be able to enjoy many outdoor high-energy and mobility-demanding activities in life, say, with your children, and to accept that you may end up sick later in life and maybe even die prematurely, perhaps even in very physically painful conditions. Those would be some of the costs of deciding you are not losing 150 pounds of excess weight, for example.

In other aspects of your life you could make a list just like this one and ponder the real cost of not living in balance because "I am too busy," "I have more important things to do," "I don't have time or money" or "I will do it later when X, Y, and Z are better".

THE WHEEL EXERCISE

Okay, let's do it!

Option 1: You may to go to my website and do this exercise online and obtain immediate results.

Option 2: From my website, www.zenbusinesswarrior.com/wheeloflife, download the form for this exercise and fill it out.

Option 3: Grab a paper and pen and do it right now.

Here is an illustration of the Wheel. There are ten main areas in your life. You will choose on a scale from one to ten (ten being the highest, meaning you are completely satisfied about how an area shows up in your life, and one, on the other end, is the complete opposite).

The first graph is the Wheel of Life for you to fill up and the second graph is an example of how it looks like after finishing the exercise. See next page.

TEN MAIN AREAS OF YOUR WHEEL OF LIFE

Take a brief moment to answer each of these questions. Do not over think it, just choose from one to ten whatever comes first to you mind. Follow your feelings.

1. Your Money and Finances

How comfortable do you feel about your financial situation—both present and future?

2. Your Emotional and Mental State

How would you rate your overall peace of mind, emotional stability, and minute-to-minute psychology?

3. Your Actions, Your Daily Choices, Your Discipline Skills

How effectively do you meet and complete each outcome you set for yourself each day?

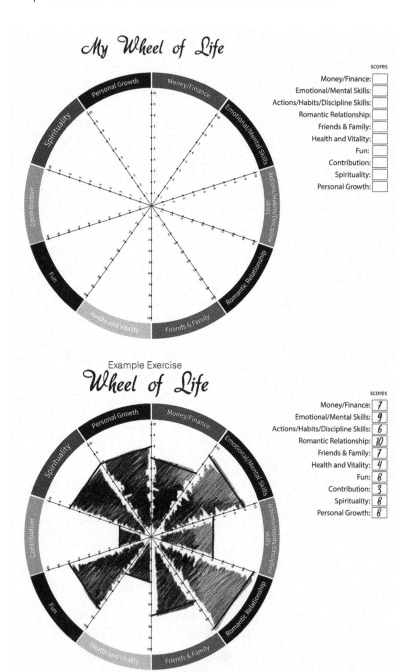

4. Your Romantic Relationship

How would you rate the overall quality of your current intimate relationship? If you are not currently in an intimate relationship, please rate your past or most recent relationship.

5. Your Friends and Family

Do you have friends and family that make you feel supported and appreciated?

6. Your Health and Vitality

How happy are you with your overall health, vitality, and the general state of your physical body?

7. Fun

How often do you plan activities *you* love for fun and relaxation?

8. Contribution

How happy are you in your ability to lead, help, and contribute to the lives of others?

9. Spirituality

How connected do you feel to something bigger than yourself? How close to do feel to finding the purpose of your life?

10. Personal Growth

How actively do you pursue activities that improve awareness of yourself, that teach you how to enhance the quality of your life and how to realize your dreams and aspirations?

How did you do? What are the areas in your life with nine or ten scores? It is now time to pat yourself on the back and say well done for these!

What are the areas that need a bit of improvement? What are the areas you marked one or two that need a lot of attention now?

This is your map. The rest is up to you.

Decide what's next and *Just do it!* —courtesy of Nike!

Chapter 7

STEP 6–ACTION
ONE DAY VS. DAY ONE

YOUR TOOLBOX

Congratulations! You have reached all the way here!

Know that this is your first step: the desire for more. You know within you that you deserve more, that you want more, and in the wanting of it, your energy—the frequency of your desire—made you have a thought about wanting to do something about it and that thought turned into an impulse to look for self-help books, or seminars, or anything to help you close the gap between where you are and where you really want to be.

That impulse then turned into the action of searching, and while you were asking a particular frequency emanated from you. You became a powerful magnet and that frequency attracted to you a frequency that is the same of that that you are asking for: this book.

91

My dear friend, if this book is in your hands it is because you and I are sharing the same frequency of desire to become more, to enjoy the journey, to have it all, right now. You are reading this book, and no other, because here you will find inspiration that will help you take the steps you need and want to take.

I want to tell you now, it will be a journey. Sometimes it will flow with ease and sometimes it will not. It is all well as it is, at any given time. It is just well, know that.

You are everything you wish to become. Everything you want to have you have already. Everything you want to do already exists. It does, you need to believe this with all your heart and soul. Remember my tip to you? "What if this were really like this…?"

All you need to do is align with your higher self. And this only means to always look for the good feeling state regardless of your present situation and "what-is-conditions."

"What-is-conditions" is old news anyway!

Yes, everything you see now around you, absolutely everything you are experiencing that you may not like or that you love in your life, you created a long time ago! Today you see the manifestation, the physicality of all your *old* thoughts and feelings.

You want tomorrow to change? It can!! Anything. Just follow simple but consistent steps to shift your energy, shift your vibrations, and your life will shift. There is no other way, it is Law. It has worked all your life for you; it has been in action. Maybe not in the intentional way you wanted, because you did not know how deliberate you can really be. But now you know. The possibilities are at your fingertips. When I say you may create anything and everything you desire, believe it, we live in a Universe of endless possibilities, we just need to choose well.

There is a challenge. The challenge is that we have been talking about feelings, emotions, energy, vibration, point of attraction, what do they all have in common? Well, what they all have in common is that you can't physically see, hear, or touch them.

The challenge of losing weight or increasing the size of your muscles is a challenge that, just the same, requires your time, your commitment, and your constancy. The easy part is that you immediately see physical tangible results. Even from the first day you start looking and feeling better

But, when it comes to exerting the Muscle of Happiness and the Muscle of Manifesting the Life you Desire… well, you may not see the results right away. It takes momentum, especially if you have been beating the low vibe drum for such a long time it has become your regular, base point of emotion and attraction.

You will need to get out of this first, to be able to get to the higher delicious states of being, states of feeling, where all the magic happens. Some call it miracles, some call it coincidences, some call it good luck, I like to call it magic because literally, just like a magician, someday your biggest-ever business account can just knock on your door. It happened to me, so I love to call it magic! (It appears to be magic … but now you know the inside story:-)

Can you do this? Of course! According to a study released in the *European Journal of Social Psychology*, it takes sixty-six days to create a new habit. Make today your day one.

BECOMING THE ZEN BUSINESS WARRIOR AT HEART

By now you are taking steps toward becoming the Master of Yourself, Master of Your Life. We are all Apprentices and Masters at any given moment in our lives. Some areas or skills we master through repetition (because we love to do them) and in some other areas we are apprentices. As either a Master or an Apprentice, you will need a toolbox filled with tools that will best allow you to master anything.

I love cooking, for instance. I am rather known in my circle of friends for being able to cook delicious dishes with apparently "no ingredients" and at amazing speed, so they say. Yeah, okay, I can do that all right, first because I love cooking so much I've had a lot of practice, second because I have experimented so much on my own and with other people's recipes that the mixing and matching comes to me easily, and last but not least importantly, because I have tools that enable me to do it at a much faster pace.

I love my Vitamix blender, so versatile! And even if I have a powerful food processor I just adore my basic, manual vegetable chopper! A big part of cooking is cutting and dicing—not a very sophisticated thing to do but time consuming and tedious. I have the right tools, and for me cooking is not a long process—which is the deterrent to begin to learn for a lot of people I know. "I spend two hours when I want to cook a nice meal. No way will I do that every day," they say.

Get the right tools, I say to my friends. I can cook a five-course meal for my family of four in less than thirty minutes (Watch out, Rachael Ray, here I come! I love her cooking TV show for the same reason: delicious and fast).

So, the same goes for the tools you will need to get to the place where everything happens with ease and where you feel the most alignment, peace, and joy. These tools help you get there faster, making it fun, not into a tedious, repetitive task you need to do.

So, here they come, the processes that have worked their magic in my life and in the life of millions of people who have made them part of their lives. They are worth ten times the time you invest in them and once you make the decision to incorporate them into your life you will see spectacular changes in your vibration, your emotion, and your mental mindset, therefore in what you attract and create in your life.

Why call it exercise, process, step, point, principle ... when life can be a Big Fun Game! These will be your Top Ten Fun and Zen Power-Tools.

ZEN POWER TOOL #1
SET THE RIGHT INTENTION

Say: "What I am about to do will be fun. I will enjoy every minute of it simply because I declare it so." Smile. That's it.

ZEN POWER TOOL #2
PRIME YOUR DAY

You are an entrepreneur; you know what the right planning means to a project. When in a project you establish the order in which events will happen and how the resources will be used (time, people, money). You most likely will reach the results intended in the project.

You will have variance for sure, but you will get back on track if you have a predefined track; if you don't have a plan, you will end up improvising every step of the way as things just come your way, and it can feel really messy and stressful. You prime your project when you do your Project Planning before you start.

Fifteen minutes is all it takes to prime your day. Your *power* resides in the *now*. Every single new day is your opportunity to create in your present time. If you prime every single day, you are allocating your resources (energy, vibration, intention, connection, alignment, mood, clarity, wisdom, love, gratitude, understanding, patience, determination, serenity, leadership, resilience ... and on and on). *These are your internal resources* to do your Life Project.

These fifteen minutes spent in priming your day is time you will best spend throughout the day in order to have easier access to all of your internal resources.

You will find with practice what makes you feel the best. I would recommend you pick one when you begin and stick to it for the first thirty days, hopefully option one or two. Option three is your go-to option when you are in a bind for time—just don't stop your practice.

Like Tony Robbins says, "If you don't have fifteen minutes for yourself, you don't have a life."

Option 1 (Ideally Fifteen Minutes Daily)

Ten Minutes Meditation and Breathing

Set a ten-minute timer. Close your eyes in a calm space, take one long breath and a longer exhale. Sit straight in a chair, hands on your lap. Just place your attention in a particular sound, even maybe your breath, or look for an app with a background sound you like, like water flowing, waves, or breeze. There will be thoughts, just let them come in and out— emptying the mind is not the purpose. Any time you get distracted, just calmly redirect your attention to the sound. Be patient and loving with yourself.

Every time it will get easier and it will feel so soothing you will not want to go a day without it, trust me.

Four Minutes Gratitude Journal

In a medium-sized journal, fill two pages every day. Take a long breath in and a longer exhale out. Say "thank you" ten times in a slow, deliberate way, feeling the energy of those words. On your left page you will have your Gratitude Now. Fill it by making a list of everything you are grateful for *in your life now*. Start from the general to the specific and always write it in the present tense: "I am grateful to be alive today," "Thank you for the beautiful day, the sun is shining." On your right page you will have your Gratitude Intentions. Fill it by making a list of *all of the things you want to come into your life*. Remember to write them as though you have them now, and begin each sentence in the same way: "I am truly grateful for …" or "I am so grateful now that … " or "Thank you for … " or any other similar words of gratitude that feel good to you.

One-Minute Setting Your Day Outcomes

Every day, make it a habit to feel the feelings of gratitude in advance for the great day ahead, as though it is done. Say or write how you want your day to be, the good news you are expecting, the good feeling you will have throughout the day and finish with "all is well at it is, as it will be."

Option 2 (Ideally Ten Minutes Daily)

Ten-Minute Heart Coherence Exercise

The Heart Math Institute has studies showing the no short of miraculous results when you create a state of coherence between your Mind and your Heart. It helps to immediately release stress, it stops draining emotions such as fear, anger, frustration, irritation, and anxiety. When you are in a coherent state, your thoughts and emotions are balanced and you experience ease and inner peace.

1. Set a timer for ten minutes. Set soft background music or sounds.
2. Heart-Focus Breathing: place your hand on the area of your heart for the first minute or so to help you focus your attention there. Imagine your breath is flowing in and out of your heart or your chest area. Breathe a little slower and deeper than usual.
3. Activate a Positive Feeling: Make a sincere attempt to experience feelings such as gratitude, appreciation, or care for someone or

something in your life. Keep the list of circumstances, people, things flowing in your mind, feel and fuel all those positive feelings in your heart and in your soul. Keep going for ten minutes. Imagine your heart's light energy connecting to your brain's light energy, as if they were intertwining.

4. When the timer goes off, just smile and know you now have both your mind and heart working as one for you. This is one of the quickest ways to turn on your sixth sense: your intuition.

Option 3 One Minute (No excuses here!)

When you only have one minute: *The Lost Mode Prayer*

Gregg Braden, one of my favorite mentors (so much fun to hear him speak), has brought to us from the ancient scrolls the "lost mode of praying." He reminds us that prayer is perhaps one of the most ancient and mysterious of human experiences, and it is also one of the most personal, since it varies by culture, religion, and traditions.

The *Lost Mode Prayer* is a prayer that is based solely in feeling. A feeling-based prayer simply invites us to feel a clear and powerful feeling as if our prayers have already been answered.

All you need to do for one minute is to close your eyes and imagine what you are feeling right now that you can see yourself, for example, healed or with a bursting bank account or with a loving new life partner by your side or enjoying your dream vacation or anything that you desire. What does it feel like? And put it into feelings for one minute.

When I think of financial abundance I feel the following: "*Having financial abundance feels like clarity, feels like ease, feels like peace of mind, feels like fun, feels like excitement, feels like gratitude, feels like appreciation for everyone that helped me, feels like self-confidence and love, feels like being able to help others, feels really good, feels like a warm feeling in my heart....* "And on and on I can go. I just love it!

ZEN POWER TOOL #3
CLARITY

To have clarity is to be halfway there.

Clarity is a powerful creating vibration. When you know without a doubt what you want, all you need to do next is align and the hows will start to show up and impulse to action will flow from you naturally.

The best way there is to clarify the path is to sit down, do a brief alignment process, and answer the following questions. Begin to write, don't stop, get the momentum going. At the end you can revise it, but start and move on. Get yourself a timer to do it in fifteen minutes. Do not hesitate, do not get stuck in how you will achieve it—that is completely irrelevant in this exercise. Go!

Question One: What Do You Really Want?

When you write what you want you are taking the first step toward manifesting it. You are decreeing to the Universe and to yourself what you want. Then something happens: you will see there is a gap between what you want and where you want to be.

Great! You may feel uncomfortable when you see the gap, all good, you are in the right track, that discomfort and unease feeling you have in your stomach only means you really care about what you wrote, it has an emotional pull on you, it can make you move your butt. Write down five things you want to see in your life. Great, next!

Question Two: Why Do You Really Want It?

When you get absolutely clear as to why this goal is a must for you, you will find your purpose. And when you are clear about your purpose it even transcends your specific goal. *The purpose of a goal is not so you can get the result, it's what the end result will make you as a person.*

This type of clarity, purpose-based goal, will keep you going, no matter if you hit a rough spot on your road. Ultimately, material objects, titles or awards will not make you happy. *The only thing that will make you happy is the person you have become and what you have created in your lifetime to you and to others.*

Write down why you want each of say, five things to happen in your life, how would your life and yourself be different. What type of person do you need to become? Great, next!

Question Three: Align Yourself with Absolute Certainty

Magic begins here: trust.

Trust in yourself. Trust in your higher-self. Trust in the co-creating infinite power of the Universe. You are not alone, ever. All that you want to do, have, and be you already are in your vibrational reality. Just let it flow to you. Align. (Aligning only means to find anything at all to make you feel good in the moment. Your present self-aligns with your higher self, your true essence, who is always in a high vibration place.)

How would your life be different if you could believe 100 percent what you just read?

Believe, because it is like that. And a belief is nothing more than a thought you keep repeating, so I invite you: repeat to yourself constantly that you have permanent access to the realm of ideas, wisdom, guidance, even networking of your divine self!

So many people give up prematurely because they focus on the outcome and then stop and tell themselves, "I don't know how to do that," or "I could never achieve that." But what if you didn't have to figure out how to do it, but rather, believed that you will figure it out no matter what? That achieving your goal is not only within the realm of possibility, it could be an absolute certainty? Just imagine how that could change your life right now.

Write down that you believe all that you wrote can, and will happen. You may not believe it, but if you write it down, you are calling it to the realm of reality. What have you got to lose? Believe! Or fake it until you do, it works too!

Question Four: Repetition Is the Mother of All Skills

You cannot set goals one time, never look at them again, and then expect long-term results. People looking for a quick fix will never achieve the level of mastery required for achieving what they most desire. Reaching your goals takes focus *and* practice. You have to repeat it over and over again.

If it's a new skill you want to acquire, practice is a key part of that. Look at all performers in sports and art. Thousands of hours practicing, honing their skills—do you think Michael Jordan or Pelé stopped going to practice when they won world-known championships? If you're looking to achieve more in your business, then determine the core processes you need to shift and execute those on a regular basis. You want joy and happiness in your company and in your life? Then work on your Happiness Muscle, every day.

If you want to master anything you have to make it part of you, you need to become it. And the only way to do it is through practice. Remember, consistent practice, constant focus—this is what will result in a profound and lasting impact on your life.

Decide right now the time, place, and frequency. Schedule it—it is not real until you schedule it. If you don't, it is just a mere pondering on, "This sounds good, I will do it later …"

There is a world of difference between *one day* and *day one*. It's what separates successful people and people who want to be successful. Which one are you?

ZEN POWER TOOL #4
WHAT NEEDS TO HAPPEN THIS YEAR
FOR IT TO BE THE BEST YEAR OF YOUR LIFE?

I cannot begin to tell you the manifesting power this question has. It changed my life.

I have always, even before going to seminars and formally beginning my personal growth journey, written my goals, desires, call them even New Year's Resolutions. They gave me a sense of clarity and direction in the moment. Oftentimes, though, I would forget about them, just to check on them every and now and then, or I would see them once a year on the one day per year I would sit and go through the exercise of writing them.

Ask me how well that worked out for me. Good, I guess—it was better than writing nothing—but since I did not have my laser-focused attention, then some came to fruition and most did not.

I see now what it was about writing those goals before. They were not emotionally charged enough for me to want to permanently visualize them, think about them, and feel the excitement—they were just "great to have" but not "must have."

To me, asking the question of my dreams tied to the phrase "the best year of my life" gave me goose bumps, accelerated my heart, made me salivate.... It was exciting beyond words. Even now as I write these words, my heart is filled with excitement and anticipation. Imagine that. I have many wonderful, absolutely magnificent experiences in my life—for me to imagine the best was literally yet to come is absolutely thrilling!

Sit a moment, dream a little, or a lot: write down the five events that need to happen in your life for this to be the best year of your life. Have fun and hang on to those feelings.

ZEN POWER TOOL #5
YOUR WORD IS LAW

Nothing speaks more of your character than when you are in integrity. This means that what you think, say, and do all align. When your intention aligns with your actions.

Nothing generates more trust than being a person who stands by their word. Not by contracts or expectations, but by their word.

Make your word law, to yourself first and then to others. There is power in just saying it *"My Word is Law."*

ZEN POWER TOOL #6
GOLD NUGGETS

Enhance your life with phrases that provide special meaning to your life.

They will remind you of the wisdom you have learned in your journey or they can help you attain the wisdom you wish to live in a particular area of your life.

Words are powerful. Words are energy and they can uplift you at a moment when you need it the most. They can also inspire you and you will end up using these phrases to help, inspire, and uplift others. They reflect your innermost values. You will remember them because they resonate with you.

At our *Familia ALO* Events we always give out wallet-sized plastic cards with the company's values on one side and our Ten Life Enhancing Gold Nuggets on the other. I would like to share them with you.

1. I love my life! (our most used affirmation in our family. Our children say it right away when asked, "How you doin'?" in an attempt at Joey's accent from the TV show Friends)
2. I create my life. My thoughts, feelings and choices create my reality.
3. My life is the result of 10 percent of what happens to me and 90 percent how I react to it.

4. What I focus on expands. What I resist, persists.
5. I take action. I correct and continue. Forward.
6. Everything happens for a reason, and that reason is always there to serve me.
7. My word is Law. It is the signature of my character.
8. Lucrative opportunities always come my way.
9. I am grateful for everything I have in my life NOW.
10. I deserve abundance because I add value to other people's lives.

My personal favorite:
"I already AM all that I wish to do, all that I want to have, and all that I desire to become. I just need to align with that higher-self part of me."

I am Serenity.

I am Clarity.

I am Wisdom.

I am Love.

I am Abundance.

ZEN POWER TOOL #7
CONTRIBUTE

Success without fulfillment is the ultimate failure.

How many times have you known of someone who apparently has everything yet is not happy? They are where they want to be in terms of all the things they asked for, yet you hear them say that happiness remained elusive. They ask themselves, "Is this all there is?"

Can you succeed in life and still not be fulfilled? Yes. When our goals only serve ourselves, then achieving our goals will only make us happy for a moment … a very short moment.

Living a fulfilled life does not happen overnight. Like the best wine it takes time. It is an art, like the artist that sculpts a masterpiece, bit by bit.

Two things need to happen to live a fulfilled life: first we must grow, we must transform, we must become more in the process. Then we must go beyond our selves and serve others. In a nutshell: what will make you feel fulfilled is to grow and to give.

When you learn the art of fulfillment, in growing and serving, you create extraordinary lives for yourself, your family, and others. When we created our Culture of Delivering Happiness in ALO, it gave us extraordinary feeling of purpose and fulfillment.

ZEN POWER TOOL #8
SOMETHING NEW

Life is fun—keep it fun! Don't fall into boring routines, do something different out of the blue for no reason.

Simply take a bike ride around where you live with no destination. Stop at a restaurant you don't know on the way to the one you know. Don't run to your car when it is raining in the parking lot, look up and enjoy the drops of water falling on your face. Get in touch with someone you have not talked to in twenty years—Facebook is great for that! Go to a hotel fifteen miles from where you live for the weekend. Decide on that gardening or decorating project you have been postponing. Print new pictures and change the ones you've been displaying for the past five years. Invite your children to a pizza restaurant on a Monday during the school week.

Well, these have been some of the things I have been doing over the past thirty days! Make a fun list of what lights you up and do it! Surprise yourself, surprise your spouse, surprise a friend, or delight your children.

ZEN POWER TOOL #9
CELEBRATE!

When was the last time you celebrated like crazy? Celebrating something you have accomplished is a sign of gratitude. It feels really good to celebrate and just burst with the emotion of it! And to share it with others.

Oftentimes we don't celebrate our small wins—sometimes not even the big ones! What are you telling the Universe? We need to celebrate more often to step in that type of energy. It feels fantastic anyway and it feels like you are on track, spot on.

But here, try this on: you don't need an excuse to feel good. You can just celebrate for no reason, just feel good for no reason. You know, the opposite is totally true for a lot of people: they feel bad for no real reason. Have you been there? Sure, we all have. "Just not having a good day," we say.

Okay, so then decide that you don't need an excuse to feel good. Smile, think about anything that you like, and celebrate. It is actually very easy: you just need to stand up, put your hands up, and jump up and down fifteen times screaming at the top of your lungs, "yeeaaaaayyyy!!!" Try it, you may even like it! The scientific truth is that your body will release feel-good hormones automatically, just because you put your body in motion. Don't be shy, try it, your kids will love it!

ZEN POWER TOOL #10
CONTINUOUS PERSONAL GROWTH

It's okay to acknowledge that you can't create a personal growth plan all on your own and stick to it. Turn to the best personal growth books, rely on personal growth quotes, or find a mentor who can help you empower yourself, help remind you who you really are, and inspire you to take continuous action in the pursuit of becoming, of being the best you can be.

If you can't access a mentor, identify someone you admire and study their choices. As Tony Robbins has said, "If you want to be successful, find someone who has achieved the results you want and copy what they do and you'll achieve the same results." How did they find success? How do they approach their daily responsibilities? Remember:

"Success leaves clues"
—Tony Robbins

By using tools and tapping into the success of others, you'll more easily develop your own path to success.

Keep growing, keep oxygenating your mind, your soul. What you watch, hear, read every day is what you are feeding yourself. Closely evaluate it. Those are your seeds. Are you planting beautiful fruit trees or are you letting weed seeds take on your garden? Be the gardener, chose the seeds, water them, watch them grow, and enjoy the fruits!!

Make the choice to grow every day.

GET SET, READY, SCHEDULE IT!

It will only be real when you schedule it.

If it is not scheduled, it is only a good intention … and you know what happens to good intentions many times, right? So go ahead, take ten minutes now, and schedule your next steps: the next ten days are critical. Whatever you don't do in the next ten days, the odds of you not doing anything at all are totally against you—trust me on this one. Turn the chance of your success in your favor right now by taking action, massive action: one step at a time.

So, you are almost done.

You have identified the gaps between where you are and where you want to be. If you want to live the life you desire, it's time to decide, commit, and resolve. It's not about what you *can* do, it's about what you *will* do.

Decide.

You know where you have gaps. Now, decide what you want to achieve.

Commit.

Eliminate fear and self-doubt. Commit fully to your goal and all the negative chatter will fall to the side.

Resolve.

No matter the obstacles, persevere to overcome any challenge to achieve your goal.

Schedule it.

"Knowledge isn't power, it's potential power.
Massive Action is Power."
– Tony Robbins

Chapter 8

STEP 7-TRUST AND FAITH LISTEN TO YOUR HEART

WHAT IF ... THIS WAS TRUE?

My invitation to you right now: allow yourself to be open-minded, to apply the best state of mind I know you can have to learn concepts that may be new to you.

Say to yourself: *"What if this was true, what if these concepts are the way things really are?"*

You've heard and read the many real-life examples of people that said they never dreamed how crazy good their lives were going to get. People like Oprah, Tony Robbins, soccer player Ronaldo, Colombian singer Shakira, fighter Connor McGregor, CEO of Salesforce Marc Benioff, rapper Jay Z ... when asked in interviews, none of them imagined, much less planned, such levels of business success.

Do you believe for a second it was good luck? Or that they were born under a good star? Or that they had a rich uncle who introduced them around?

Not at all. Each of them created their lives. They all had things in common: a burning desire and powerful thoughts and feelings that carried them forward, until they gained momentum (keep this in mind, big word, bigger implication, coming up later), little by little at first, then it poured in torrents of success, wealth, and fame.lunch

We, from the outside, only see the end result, but it took enormous emotional strength from their part and Grace from the Universe and the co-creating components they summoned to their lives through their empowering beliefs and sustained positive emotions.

The only way they could do it was because they had powerful thoughts to hold on to when crap hit the fan—because it does hit the fan every now and then, it happens to everybody—it is where contrasts are born and it is the moments when you have the best clarity in your life. The only thing they did differently is how they handled it when things went south. And they did, very well indeed.

WHO AM I? SECOND PART

About Vibrations

Okay, so we are officially going to start getting to *The Zone,* as I would like to call it.

For those who know me, yes, I am by training and experience an executive, meaning I execute things in my business and I have done it for other big shot enterprises. I am totally at ease with the formal structure and jargon of that world—I even like it. That is my disclaimer.

Now, let's get really interesting here, past the text book concepts about beliefs, fears, pleasure, and how you push or pull yourself. Don't get me wrong, that is all important for you to understand and for you to do.

What follows here though is what for me has been determinant in our successes and our failures. And it is what makes me tick, it is what I believe to the core of my being has worked in my business and in my life. Besides, once you are past the understanding and believing, it is the easiest and most fun of all paths!

GRACE: *Trust* in the Divine, the Intangibles, and the Laws of the Universe

To recap: we are at our core emotional beings, not intellectual beings. Then it is fair to say we are ruled by our emotions (please don't freak out here, I know you are a level-headed, responsible, determined, rational businessperson). These emotions then elicit subconscious responses that turn into decisions in order to seek pleasure or avoid pain (all in our minds, not in the immediate physical sense of the words).

Let me add now to this definition.

Human beings, you and me, are made of energy. We are part of a Universe that is made of energy. Every single particle in the Universe, including us, is energy. Remember Einstein? Yes, E=MC2, confirms without a shred of scientific doubt what you just read—I know you are with me here.

Energy is made of vibration, vibrations that resonate at different frequencies.

The typical example of a frequency is that of radio transmitter: if you want to listen to classical music you will tune-in to the AM frequency 101.2 for classical music. If you tune in to the frequency of 102.1 by intention or mistake you will listen to heavy metal music instead.

Therefore, *being an Emotional Being means that you are a Vibrational Being.*

Being a Vibrational Being means you vibrate at either low or high frequencies.

Everything that you see around you is focused vibrations. Everything vibrates at a specific level that gives the characteristics that you, through *your vibration sensors,* can then intake and translate in your brain to be able to see, hear, touch, and taste all that you experience. Love is vibration-based, so is money, so is health, so is your daily cereal and your dog. All.

YOUR FEELINGS: *YOUR CREATIVE ABSOLUTE POWER*

Your feelings are vibrations.

They can be very powerful, supportive, and serve you well or they can destroy you and your life and those you love with it. You can even choose a slow or a quick death depending on the regularity and intensity of the feeling you most often feel. A bit gory?

In your vibrational reality, you can either thrive or die (you may still be breathing, but that does not really make a difference). I just wanted to make a very quick and unforgettable point.

Your emotions come in a wide variety of frequencies, from the highest vibrations like love, appreciation, and gratitude to the lowest vibrations like fear, depression, and anger. The higher the frequency of your energy or vibration, the lighter you feel in your physical, emotional, and mental body.

When you appreciate an employee for a job well done, you are feeling appreciation, which is high vibration frequency. When you feel overwhelmed with the amount of things you need to do in your business, and you are feeling despair and frustration, these are low vibration frequencies.

The feelings in your life are the creators of your experience. They are the magnets that attract to your life the situations, circumstances, and people that you want ... or don't want.

In the absolutely awe-inspiring and very concise book *As a Man Thinketh* by James Allen (written more than a 120 years ago), he tells us *"that which is like unto itself, is drawn."* In other words, that which you think, in any moment, attracts unto itself other thoughts that are like it.

This means that you are a *powerful magnet*: your energy, the frequency of your feelings, will attract to you the exact same frequency of things, people, and circumstances that you are feeling. If you feel anger, you will have more situations that will make you angry. If you feel fearful for lack of money, you will have more situations that will decrease the inflow of money and continue making you afraid of lack of money … and so on.

And at the same time, the fantastic wonderful news is that it works just as perfectly the other way around. If you feel appreciation, you will have more things to appreciate. If you feel excited, fantastic new ventures will literally knock on your door. You will think they are "coincidences," but they are not!

All good things come to you when you expect them to show up. You will wake up in the morning excited, eager with positive anticipation to find out what you will bring to your day.

In the book *Think Rich and Grow Rich* by Napoleon Hill, the author invites us to reflect once again on how very determinant to our experience our thoughts are: both for good or for bad.

Allow me to share with you powerful quotes from this life-transforming book:

"When you begin to think and grow rich, you will observe that riches begin with a state of mind, with definiteness of purpose, with little or no hard work. You, and every other person, ought to be interested in knowing how to acquire that state of mind which will attract riches…. Observe very closely, as soon as you master the principles of this philosophy, and begin to follow the instructions for applying those principles, your financial status will begin to improve, and everything you touch will begin to transmute itself into an asset for your benefit. Impossible? Not at all!"

Success comes to those who become success conscious. Failure comes to those who indifferently allow themselves to become failure conscious.

… that before we can accumulate riches in great abundance, we must magnetize our minds with intense desire for riches, that we must become 'money conscious' until the desire for money drives us to create definite plans for acquiring it."

THE SAME QUESTION, AGAIN:
ARE YOU ASKING INTELLIGENTLY?

Another very important issue: the language of the Universe, so to speak, is that of vibration, *not words*. This means: when you ask with positive words what you want, *but* what you really feel is the lack of what you are asking, the Universe listens and sends your way what you are feeling!

So, if you ask for money loud and clear: "I would like to have more money in my life to be able to care for myself and my loved ones and have a better life" *but* if, when you say these words and what you really feel is a sense of lacking money, of scarcity and fear, then that is what you are shouting out and asking for from the Universe.

NOT JUST "POSITIVE" OR "NEGATIVE" FEELING

I really don't like to label any feeling as positive or negative, because I believe that all feelings show you where you are in regards to what you are creating in your life right in the moment. They are your guiding system.

So if something is of use to you, how can it be negative?

Let me share what I do: if I am feeling fear about a particular situation, I just stop and acknowledge the feeling, the "negative" feeling. I then say to myself: "Mmm … okay, you are afraid, not good. *First,* you don't want that which you are fearing to come into your life, so stop right now." *Second,* I closely examine my thoughts regarding that fear. 100 percent of the time I am fearing something not real—I repeat, something not real, it has not happened. Once I regain my peace of mind I then proceed to plan what to do about it and I do it!

The huge difference here is that I am now acting from a place of expecting a solution (creating and attracting the change I expect) and not from a place of panic and fear (avoiding what I fear is going to happen).

YOUR EMOTIONAL GUIDANCE SCALE

There is a wide range of emotions and having a mental picture of a scale will help recognize where you are to move to a higher vibrating scale little by little.

The better you feel throughout the day, the more you are allowing the creation of all the things you desire. When you feel great this is what you are really telling yourself:

- *That you are free.*
- *That you are powerful.*
- *That you are good.*
- *That you are love.*
- *That you have value.*
- *That you have purpose.*
- *That all is well.*

This Emotional Scale is given to us by Abraham Hicks/Esther Hicks. In almost all their books they refer to this emotional scale. I have found it of enormous value to me to be able to see a particular emotion on a scale. When I see that at the very bottom is fear, I pinch myself out of this illusion every time I feel it, because that is what fear is: a complete illusion of something that has happened only in your head, that is not real.

Now if you keep thinking about it, it will be real. You will create the physical evidence of your most recurring thoughts and then say, "I knew this was going to happen!" But to be very clear: *It did not happen to you, you made it happen.* You gave it life with your thoughts that turned into magnetic emotions, that decided the course of your actions and those around you and then the results showed themselves. It is a Universal Law and it is called Law of Attraction.

EMOTIONAL SCALE

How close you are to the higher vibrating emotions will determine how close you are to your absolute powerful creating power. You are a magnificent being, all that you want to become, you already are, you are an eternal being, you are wise beyond what you think.

When you hear about old and wise sages of the world, it is about the experience and how they have given it meaning, but experience only comes with years.

Imagine for a second: you are an eternal being, your soul is eternal, how much experience could you have? How much wisdom? All you need to do is connect to that higher self, and the connection is through your emotions, through your feelings. This is when the word *intuition* comes in. You have a *feeling,* you don't know where it comes from … but you know. How many times has this happened to you? We need to learn to trust our intuition, it is powerful and it is always available to us, any time we need it.

WHAT IS YOUR POINT OF CREATION? OF ATTRACTION?

First, let's take a look at your *base emotional state.*

This is the feeling you most easily go to in any situation.

I was once at a Tony Robbins event and he had an intervention with a woman who was strongly reacting to the September 11 attacks. She was really very angry, she kept on going and going. When Tony asked

Your Emotional Guidance Scale
HIGH VIBRATION

HIGH POSITIVE FEELINGS
(The Better it Gets, The Better it Gets!)

+7	Joy/Appreciation/Empowered/Freedom/Love
+6	Passion
+5	Enthusiasm/Eagerness/Happiness
+4	Positive Expectation/Belief
+3	Optimism
+2	Hopefulness
+1	Contentment
0	Neutral Low Emotion
-1	Boredom
-2	Pessimism
-3	Frustration/Irritation/Impatience
-4	Overwhelm
-5	Disappointment
-6	Doubt
-7	Worry
-8	Blame
-9	Discouragement
-10	Anger
-11	Revenge
-12	Hatred/Rage
-13	Jealousy
-14	Insecurity / Guilt/ Unworthiness
-15	Fear/Grief/ Depression/Despair/Powerlessness

Feeling Good / Good Alignment →

Feeling Bad / Bad Alignment

LOW NEGATIVE FEELINGS
(The Worse it Gets, the Worse it Gets!

her if she was American, she said no. When Tony asked her if she lived in New York, she said no. When Tony asked her if she lost someone in the attack, she said no. Any organization she belongs to? No again … He was a bit baffled, then went on to make a brilliant point: her reaction was based on her Base Emotional State.

When asked if she was prompt to get angry and reactive, she paused and said yes. Clearly she was just coming from her base emotional state. She had no direct emotional link to the September 11 attacks but her level of outrage was out of proportion to the discussion.

What is your base emotional state? When the going gets tough and even in not-so-challenging situations, like a level two problem: do you usually get angry? Do you usually just withdraw to your corner? Do you start criticizing all that is wrong and when you least expect it, turn it into an avalanche of garbage coming out of your mouth, even surprising you? Do you start self-flagellating with no mercy? What are your most go-to-feelings?

Watch very carefully, because your base emotional state, that which is so close to your surface, is your point of creation, your point of vibration. That is the type of magnet you have turned on all the time, whether intentional or not.

YOUR THOUGHTS

The next determinant variable: where do your feelings come from? Your thoughts.

Your power resides in the ability you can develop to sustain focus of thoughts that make you feel good. If I could right now make you read these lines twenty times until you memorize them, I would. This is one of the most powerful concepts you can take from this book.

You are the creator of your life.

*"We are not Physical Beings having a Spiritual Experience. We are
Spiritual Beings having a Physical Experience."*
– Teilhard Chardin

You create your life. All of it.

Whether you like it or not, you have created the outcomes in your life.

Whether you think it is fair or not, you have created them.

Whether you do it intentionally or not, you have created them.

I know you are thinking, "I can't possibly have created the fraud that almost broke my company a few years ago, or the employee that stole money from me, or the account that never paid us almost $50,000 in bills, or my sickness, or my depression?" Yes, there is no one that has more at stake in all these than you. It is in your best self-interest that all you do produces the results you want and that you work so hard for.

Still, crap happens, right? Some days, at least.

Why? I will say it again: you are the creator of it all. Yes, when I was fired, when I lost my properties, when my company was at the edge of going down, the big two money frauds we've had, all of it: my creation. Did I want it, did I like it? Noooo!! Am I pounding my chest with *Mea Culpa* and feeling rotten about it? No. Am I blaming others, the government, the Universe, my employees, my competitors, my dog that ate my homework? No.

Did I learn? Heck yes! The lesson was not only on a technical level: better investment insights to pull out in time, better business insights about being a true expert of a particular product and having raving fans vs. becoming an expert-in-formation in many products, no matter how innovative they appeared to look, and un-focusing our company for two years.

MY LIFE'S LESSON—CRYSTAL CLEAR

My true lesson was about deeply looking back, with an X-ray honesty and with a compassionate take about my emotional mindset during that time. What was I feeling then? And what were the thoughts that created those feelings on a permanent basis? What actions did I take based on those feelings? What did I *really* attract to my life?

I am the creator of my life, it is 100% my responsibility. The big question to always bear in mind is how we actually create the end results, how we manifest what happens, big or small, good or bad.

Witnessing, connecting the dots between my feelings and my living reality, I was able to clearly see how all the aspects in my life I felt really good about, grateful about, like my deep relationship with David, my wonderful relationship with my children, my vibrant health and fit body, our loving and harmonious life at home, my fun-filled relationship with our friends and the love and support in our extended family, our life filled with new and exciting experiences … all these areas were abundant and fulfilling in my life.

But—*and a big but, my friends, and the true moment of truth in this book*—when I look back at our company's finances and growth over those years, I can clearly see now a totally different story: feelings of anxiety over not meeting our sales budget, overwhelming feelings of frustration, daily outbursts of fear-based anger when problems were inundating our desks, feelings of disappointment and despair every time we lost an important customer or a key employee left, and most of all it felt like I was in a fog, doing a million things but not having a clear sense if they were focused in the right direction.

It was never about not taking action, or even the wrong action.

Everything happening in our lives was directly linked to our most permanent thoughts and thus, feelings in the moment. Then, it gained momentum, for good or for bad. It is crystal clear and I am very sure that if you do this same exercise you will notice the same in your life.

We are entrepreneurs, *we take actions, make decision,* all the time!

Our biggest mistake: to disregard completely this relationship of cause and effect. We feel bad or good *and then* bad or good *will* happen, *not* the other way around.

I truly believe that if David and I did not have the knowledge and tools I have shared with you in this book, our company would have closed during that time, affecting our lives and the lives of those we love and care for.

I learned many invaluable lessons, all of which I am immensely grateful for. They have shaped me and make me a better version of myself.

I learned to be very conscious of my beliefs, my thoughts, my feelings, my actions and then my results. I work on them everyday.

There are no big surprises now. When something I don't really like happens, I look within; when I want something to really happen, I look within. I assess what I am feeling, then I shift. Then, and only then, I act.

This is a skill that can be learned, with repetition, as any Master would say, is about practice, repetition, correcting, forgiving yourself when needed and always looking to become more in the process, to enjoy the journey.

I decided to take this path, knowing it would be step by step. And I asked for help, in the form of books, audiobooks, coaches who became my accountability partners, seminars, youtube videos, podcasts … anything that to keep my blade sharp, my heart whole, and my momentum fresh and strong. It is never a one things does it all.

WHO ARE YOU REALLY?

- *You are a magnificent eternal being.*
- *You are a powerful creator.*
- *You are free.*
- *You are not alone, ever.*

- *You are wise beyond your own conscious knowledge.*
- *You are love, you are compassion, you are appreciation, that is your essence.*
- *You came here with a purpose: to live your life to its fullest expression.*

WHO YOU ARE NOT?

Every single self-loathing story, self-sabotaging manifestos, self-diminishing adjective you have created in your mind about yourself that makes you small is exactly who you are not!

If you are going to choose a story, because that is what you do every day, choose one that helps and supports you. Even if you don't believe it at first, choose and say over and over and over again that you already are everything you want to become in your physical experience.

You *already are* all you wish in your vibrational state, your eternal spirit. That larger part of you that is in the non-physical realm is everything you want to become. That is why when you say something good about yourself you feel good, and if you don't it is only because you have told yourself the complete opposite for too long!

Say something good you truly believe about yourself and you will feel really warm, happy, and good!

Say something awfully disempowering about yourself and you will immediately feel a pang and heaviness in your chest—you may even feel sick. When this happens it only means that what you are thinking is in complete opposition to what the higher-self non-physical part of you knows and feels about you.

This is your navigation system telling you that you are waaaaayyyyy off course! No action that you could take that comes from this place of feeling (powerless, afraid, overwhelmed, angry, frustrated, hopeless) will yield any positive results.

It will be like wanting to go north and sprinting with all your might to the south.

Yes, you may have the best running shoes, techniques, speed, stamina, and energy ... but you are running in the wrong direction!!

Your feelings, how you feel every moment, tell you, scream at you sometimes, if you are *on* or totally *off* your path. Okay, you will think, "So this means that Lina never feels frustrated, angry, afraid, overwhelmed? What BS!"

Let me tell you: *I do*!! But, and again a big *but* here, I don't stay there.

Very quickly I acknowledge the feeling, I look at it, I decide whether it is a delusion or not (most of the time it is), and when I feel it is not a "delusion" I might have a justification for that feeling, but I then do a very important step: I give the other person the benefit of the doubt.

I ask myself: *Why would she do that? What reasons could she have from her perspective? Did she misunderstand my intentions? Did I misunderstand her intentions? What other stories could there be to it? Maybe she is just having a really rotten day and this clouded her judgment ...* Anything to alleviate my negative feelings.

Then, third step: wait. If you can wait twenty-four hours or at least until the next day, wait. If you can't, then cool off a bit before you engage in the situation and look for ways to solve it. If you repeat this very important process, in time it becomes automatic and it will enormously help you to act instead of reacting.

There is a world of difference between these two behaviors (acting vs. reacting), and the difference can mean the quality of your life.

TRUST

Trust in Yourself – Trust in the Universe – Have Faith

You are not alone. Ever. You are part of a magnificent and powerful being that is the larger non-physical part of you and that is *one with*

Infinite Intelligence, always guiding you, always helping you. Many times carrying you.

You are part of everything that exists. We are all connected, all physical beings, all nature, all things to all that is non-physical: other magnificent beings made of light and love, like you, and we are all connected to the creative power of the universe, you may call it God, Infinite Intelligence, or whatever your spiritual or religious beliefs tells you.

When you truly contemplate the possibility that this could be true there is no limits to what you can be, do or have! *None.*

You can harness the power that creates worlds, the power that creates universes.

To this power of creation it is the same to create a button or a castle, it is the same to create ten dollars or to create ten million dollars— it is!. We—you and I and everybody else—get stuck in the "*what is of the moment,*" meaning the things and situations you are currently living, your "so-called reality." And so, we tend to also get caught in the "hows": How do I get out of this? How do I make things happen? And once again, when we feel alone and powerless, impotent to turn things around, is when we are completely forgetting that we are not alone, that we are powerful and magnificent creative beings. Just look around: so many thousands of successful and meaningful personal stories ... and they all say the same thing: "If I did it, so can you!!"

Some time ago David, was feeling a bit stressed over a couple of important business decisions he was weighing. I asked him, "How would you feel if you had in your board of directors Steve Jobs, Tony Robbins, Bill Gates, Oprah, Mandela, even Jesus Christ? And if you were to meet with them once a month and show them your plans for the company, what you have done, what you plan to do, and you ask for their recommendations, would you listen to them? Would you feel confident every month *knowing* they have your back and you can't go wrong? And if you did, and all was well, you would go back tell them about it and they could again "enlighten" you? How would that make you *feel?"*

Just the thought makes me feel invincible!! I would feel I could conquer the world! I would feel love, appreciation, and gratitude to them in ways that words cannot express! I would feel worthy, I would feel alive, I would feel loved, I would feel confident, I would feel I had clarity, I would feel certain, I would feel powerful, I would feel joy, I would feel excited, I would feel thrilled and eager to take action. *Every single day I would feel awesome!*

And you know what: *this is the way it is.*

If you choose to believe.

If you choose to trust in yourself.

If you choose to trust in all the cooperative components of the Universe and your life. *Everything is happening for you, not to you.*

You are a component of the unfolding of the creation of your life. Choose your feelings well to bring onboard other components to your personal path of least resistance creation, to the most joyous path for you.

It is your choice.

It is your power.

You are free to choose. This is your total and absolute power. Your free will is the freedom to choose your thoughts to harness the creative power of your feelings. That is what it means to have free will.

This is the power that creates words and you have access to it.

Choose well, my friend.

MY WISH FOR YOU

MAY THE FORCE OF YOUR HEART BE WITH YOU

It will be a beautiful journey, if you so choose.

Know that is all within you, that there is nothing you are lacking, nothing you are not enough for, nothing you are missing. All you need to be, you already are—let it seep through you little by little.

You are the warrior, you have proven that again and again many times over. You are that man or woman who has taken steps into the unknown, into uncertainty.

You have a brave heart that has carry you through so many of your life experiences. Now is the time to let that brave heart evolve into the *Zen Heart of the Warrior,* where all is well because you know yourself and trust in yourself, the universe, and the co-creating component of your reality. It is in your heart that your power resides, not in your mind.

Your mind has and will serve you well, but let it be the servant and not the master.

Let your brave and powerful heart be your guide until you become one with it.

It will give you the peace of mind you need, the excitement every day, the strength to carry on when you need it, the wisdom of the sages, the knowledge of the universe, and the creating power of God.

You are a magnificent being. You are.

I wish you an extraordinary life and freedom on your terms, my warrior. I dwell in love, appreciation, and gratitude for you as I write these words.

Follow the Seven Steps—they are a trail to where you want to be.

Make this year the best year of your life if you so choose and become the person you were born to be. Have the success you so well deserve and have fun and enjoyment along the way!

Lina

~So be it~

ACKNOWLEDGMENTS

Thank you to the *"I am that I am,"* who is all of us, within us, and around us. Me. All. God.

To the incessant knocking on my door from my higher self, to the part in me that finally dared to open the door and peeked out. To the part in me that being hesitant yet faithful, letting the possibility grow from a single *"giddy feeling"* to a full-blown reality, which now is just the beginning of a new beginning. A new path in my life, an unknown journey now, yet filled with the certainty of growth, joy, and fulfillment.

Has there been a book acknowledgment to one's higher self? I don't know, I've never seen one before, but what I now know for sure is that the most important relationship I will ever have in this lifetime will be with myself since I cannot give to others what I don't give myself first and I cannot be to others what I am not within me first.

The experience of writing this book has required of me to become the observant. The loving and compassionate observant that I needed to

129

be in order to "download" the inspiration and content for this book. The observant who was able to say *"It is okay, you are doing just fine, it is all good as it is. Keep on going, you know it and are living it by heart, so let it show you the way. Trust in the Universe, in yourself and in the co-creating components that have come together right now to make this happen. Trust. Take one little step a time."*

Trust must have been the single word I most repeated to myself over and over, wanting to believe to the fullest extent that all was perfect as it was coming along. The timing of it all—in the middle of *soooo* many things in my life—was just perfect. It inspired me to search every day for the best version of me in all aspects of my life.

To David, my husband, who really is the best thing that has ever happened to me in this life. This was not the exception, he supported me and gave me all the confidence and countless and loving feedback every single step of the way. I could not have done it without you. I love you.

To my favorite daughter, Tamara, and my favorite son, Daniel, the lights of my life, thank you for being my little life mirrors.

To all the teachers whose shoulders I stand upon, who have shaped my way of thinking, feeling, and being. I will remain forever grateful for having you come into my experience to inspire me to grow and become more in the process. To Angela Lauria, my coach and mentor, thank you for paving the way and showing me step-by-step how to walk into this new and totally out of my comfort zone world to show up to play bigger. It has been about the journey all along. I asked the Universe and you showed up. My immense gratitude and love to you and your extraordinary team.

To the Morgan James Publishing team: Special thanks to David Hancock, CEO & Founder for believing in me and my message. To my Author Relations Manager, Margo Toulouse, thanks for making the process seamless and easy. Many more thanks to everyone else, but especially Jim Howard, Bethany Marshall, and Nickcole Watkins.

Some months ago I was listening to one of my teachers on YouTube as part of my daily Prime the Day habit. He asked: *"What needs to happen this year, 2018, for it to be the best year of your life?"* I was ecstatic! I ran and grabbed paper and a pen. I had already written my goals for this year, but to hear it in those powerful words—*"the best year of my life"*—was beyond exciting and delicious to me! I sat and proceeded to write five things that had to happen in 2018 for it to be the best year of my life and happily folded the piece of paper and put it away.

Just a week later I was meditating outside our backyard, where we have a spectacular lake view; the day was cool and I was sitting under a beautiful tree that my daughter Tamara has named Jerry, when this question just popped into my mind again.

I then felt a jolt when these words came to my mind: *"2018 will be the best year of my life if I become who I was born to be."* I had tears rolling down my cheeks, love and appreciation flowed through my whole body with such an intensity I have felt only a few times in my life. Upon re-reading my list I realized that all five things I wrote had to do with *doing* and *having,* but not with *being.*

Less than a week later over a series of "coincidences" I had made the commitment to write this book, and here it is now.

Thank you to each of you that share the desire for a life filled with growth, joy and fulfillment.

May you have a magnificent life on your terms.

Lina

> *"Life is a journey, not a destination."*
> **– Ralph Waldo Emerson**

FURTHER READING

- Delivering Happiness—Tony Hsieh
- Secrets of the Millionaire Mind—T. Harv Eker
- Satyen Raja, https://warriorsage.com/
- Human Design and The Divine Matrix—Gregg Braden
- The Passion Test—Janet Attwood
- Think and Grow Rich—Napoleon Hill
- As a Man Thinketh—James Allen
- The Power of Awareness—Neville Goddard
- I Can See Clearly Now—Dr. Wayne W. Dyer
- You'll See It When You Believe It—Dr. Wayne W. Dyer
- Ask and It Is Given—Esther and Jerry Hicks
- Getting into the Vortex—Esther and Jerry Hicks
- The Secret—Rhonda Byrnes
- Authentic Happiness—Dr. Martin E.P. Seligman
- Awaken the Giant Within—Tony Robbins

- The Money Game—Tony Robbins
- Hiring for Attitude—Mark Murphy
- Delivering Happiness—Tony Hsieh
- The Story of Purpose—Joey Reiman
- The Lean Startup—Eric Ries
- The Key—Joe Vitale

ABOUT THE AUTHOR

 Lina Betancur is a jack of all trades and is now mastering the art of living a happy, deliberate, and fulfilled life. She believes that every day is a magnificent opportunity to create the life that we are each meant to have by rediscovering who we really are. It is a, *"Never-ending, you-can-never-get-it wrong, you-can-never-really-get-it done, thrilling way to savor the deliciousness of life as you create it!"* as you may often hear her saying.

The desire to help others knocked on her door about ten years ago when she transformed the organizational culture of her company to one of *Delivering Happiness at Work*, soon transforming it from the inside out and giving birth to their slogan "A Business with Soul," which, since then, has marked a clear difference in the way they lead the company, a difference in the way the employees work and thrive and especially a difference in their customers' experiences. This has created growth for the company, their employees, their customers, and their vendors.

This knock became more insistent, requiring her to play bigger and expand to combine her spiritual life lessons with her down-to-earth, no-nonsense way of getting things done that has marked all her professional life. Writing a book and finally extending her guiding and inspiring coaching outside of her circle of influence became the natural next step.

"It is about the journey, it is about re-discovering who you really are," she always says.

She holds a Bachelor of Science in Business Administration with a major in marketing and an MBA, is bilingual, and has experienced the diversity of living in many countries. She had a rising career for ten years in leading industry corporations and for the past fifteen years she has led, together with her husband, her company into a successful telecommunication and technology multi-portfolio B2B in the Latin-American market—a process marked with many challenges, winnings and priceless personal and entrepreneurial lessons learned. Over the past twelve years she has committed herself to personal-growth, attending and being certified with business and life masters such as Anthony Robbins, T. Harv Eker, Gregg Braden, Abraham Hicks, Wayne Dyer, and John Kehoe, among many others.

Lina is an avid reader, amateur chef, passionate traveler, proud mother of Tamara and Daniel, and partner-lover-best friend of husband David. They live in South Florida with their cat, LiliBlue.

THANK YOU!

Thanks for taking the time to read *Secrets of the Zen Business Warrior*. Many businesspeople believe that making their business grow to the levels of wealth they desire depends on titanic work, considerable financial funding, special skills and knowledge, and many times the sacrifice of the quality of their personal lives.

I find that the most powerful way to grow your business to the next level is to first grow yourself to the next level, so you can find the permanent clarity, fulfilment, passion, and motivation you will need to maintain and bring wealth and abundance of everything that is good to your life.

If that was the conclusion you reached as well, please enjoy my complimentary ACCELERATED MASTERCLASS TRAINING. I've created an intense TWENTY-MINUTE TRAINING to help you make this *your Day One* (vs. one day...).

You can get it now by going to http://www.zenbusinesswarrior.com/masterclass.

"It is a rat's race" they say. I say: *"Yes, if you let it be so."* "Busy lives" is what it is, true, but you can decide, you can actually choose how to live that busy life, one that makes you feel alive, passionate, and happy, and yes: financially abundant, too.

In the training we're going to talk about:

- How you create your life and how you can harness that force to work for you, not against you.
- How the alignment of Intention—Decision—Action, determines your results.
- The right way to connect to your powerful warrior's heart.
- Find out what your *base attraction point* is. Right now, are you in alignment with what you want to show or manifest in your life? Find out.

This is an essential part of the knowledge I teach my inner circle, to become the person we are each meant to be and live an extraordinary life on our own terms.

Get it as my gift for reading the book at
www.zenbusinesswarrior.com/masterclass

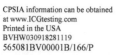
CPSIA information can be obtained
at www.ICGtesting.com
Printed in the USA
BVHW030918281119
565081BV00001B/166/P